REDISCOVERING ALBANIA

Adam Yamey *was born in England. He graduated in both physiology and dentistry at University College London. He has visited South East Europe often, and has published four books about the Balkans, including two about Albania:* "Albania on my Mind" *and* "From Albania to Sicily". *His published work also includes books and academic papers about aspects of South African history. A keen traveller and an active member of the Anglo-Albanian Association, Adam lives in London, is married, and has one daughter.*

Dedicated to the caring staff at Chelsea and Westminster Hospital, London

Copyright © Adam R Yamey 2016

Adam R Yamey has asserted his right under the Copyright, Designs and Patents Act 1988 to be identified as the author of this work.

This work is sold subject to the condition that it shall not, by way of trade or otherwise, be lent, resold, hired out, or otherwise circulated without the publisher's prior consent in any form of binding or cover other than that which it is published and without a similar condition being imposed on the subsequent purchaser.

No part of this publication may be reproduced, stored in a retrieval system, or transmitted, in any form or by any other means, electronic, mechanical, or otherwise, without prior permission of the copyright holder.

Published by Adam R Yamey

[A lulu.com project]

ISBN: 978-1-326-80710-8

www.adamyamey.com

Rediscovering

Albania

Adam Yamey

"I like the Albanians much; they are not all Turks; some tribes are Christians. But their religion makes little difference in their manner or conduct."

Lord George Byron, writing to his mother from Preveza on 12th November, 1809

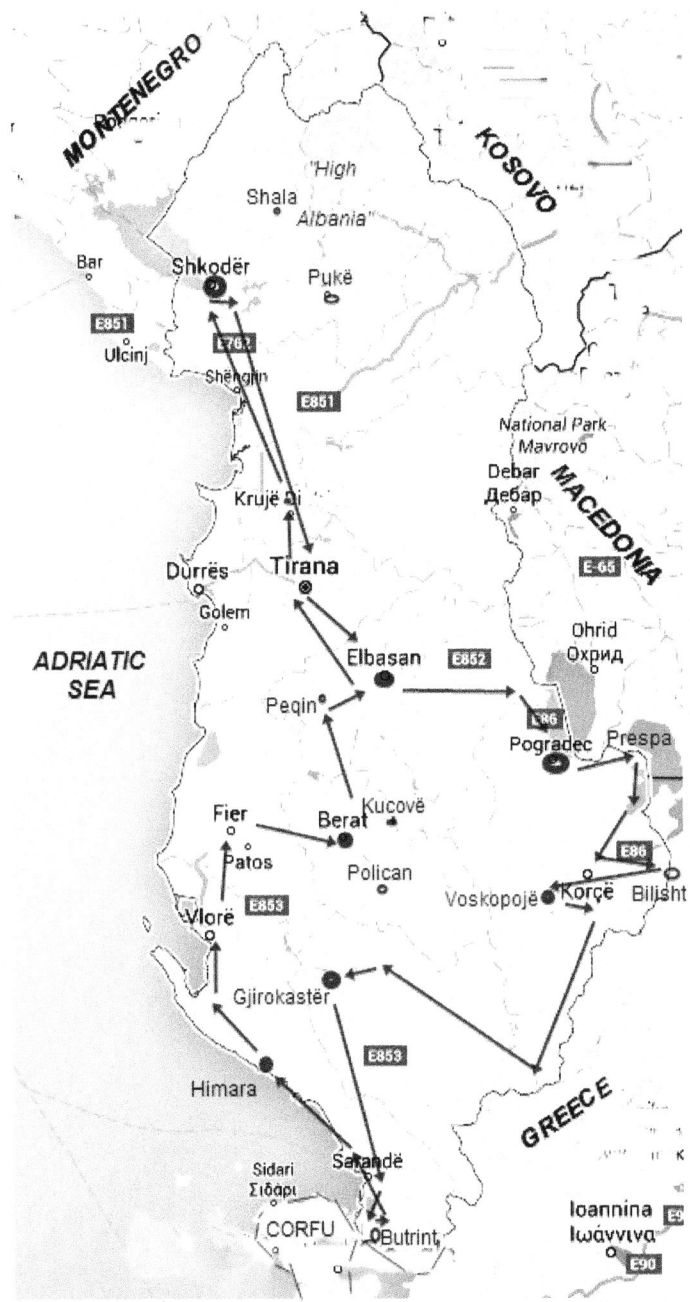

Map of Albania showing author's route, beginning and ending in Tirana
(This map does not include all places mentioned in the text)

PLACES VISITED IN ALBANIA in 2016

1. **Tirana** (3 nights) & Mount Dajti
2. Krujë, **Shkodër** (3 nights)
3. Mesi, Bogë, Shala, Koplik
4. Shirokë, Zogaj, Vau-i-dejës, Pukë
5. **Elbasan** (1 night)
6. Lin, **Pogradec** (2 nights)
7. Drilon
8. Tushemisht, Prespa, Bilisht, **Voskopojë** (3 nights)
9. Korçë
10. Dardhë, Mborje, Voskop
11. Ersekë, Petran, Përmet
12. **Gjirokastër** (2 nights)
13. Saranda, Butrint, Shën Vasil, Porto Palermo
14. Llogara, Vlorë, **Himara** (2 nights)
15. Fier, Apollonia, Ardenicë
16. Kuçovë
17. **Berat** (4 nights)
18. Poliçan, Çorovodë, Osumi Canyon, Bogova
19. Peqin
20. **Tirana** (2 nights)

*Places in **bold** are where we stayed overnight*

At the end of Spring 2016, I made a journey of discovery through one of Europe's least-known countries.

Albania, washed by the waters of the Adriatic Sea and cut-off from its Balkan neighbours by mountains and lakes, was kept isolated from the rest of the world by the dictator Enver Hoxha (1908-1985) and his officials. During the dictatorship, people outside the country's tightly guarded borders knew little about life in Albania. And those within them knew sparingly little about life beyond them.

In 1984, I went on a guided tour of Albania. It was then the only way for a tourist to visit the country. We were shown only what the Albanian government wanted us to see. Things were artfully arranged to give us what the authorities hoped was a favourable view of the country. During this fascinating trip, we were kept under constant surveillance; told not to stray from the group; prevented from speaking with any Albanians except our guides; made to eat out of sight of Albanians; and limited in what we could record with our cameras.

In February 1991, an angry crowd in Tirana attached cables around a huge statue of Albania's former dictator Enver Hoxha, one of Josef Stalin's most fervent admirers, and then they pulled on them to bring it toppling to the ground. The crowd's fury resulted from having to endure a very repressive dictatorship between 1944 and the end of 1990.

In May 2016, I returned to Albania. My wife and I hired a car. We travelled wherever we wanted; spoke with whomever we wanted (often in Italian, which is a commonly used foreign language in Albania); ate with Albanians; and photographed whatever interested us. Unhindered by security police, we explored the country. I could compare what I remembered of the country when I was there in 1984 with how it is now. From being a hermetically sealed country like North Korea is today, Albania has enthusiastically embraced the world around it.

This book has its origins in the detailed diary entries that I made at the end of each day in Albania. Using the diary as the basis for my narrative, I have added information that I have gleaned from: published material (books, journals, Internet, etc.); observations made by earlier visitors to the country; and the opinions of Albanians we met. My aim is to describe our experiences in Albania within the context of its troubled past and vibrant present.

The photographs in this volume are in black and white. I have posted many coloured pictures that I took on our journey on: https://www.facebook.com/albanian2016images/, which can be accessed without needing a Facebook account.

Now, using one of the few words of English that most Albanians know, I ask you to: "Enjoy!"

The Mangalem district of Berat

Tirana

Our journey began and ended in Albania's capital. We spent three days there before exploring the rest of the country.

When the British poet and artist Edward Lear (1812-1888) approached Tirana in September 1848, he was not bowled over. He wrote in his book, *Journals of a Landscape Painter in Greece and Albania*:

"As I advanced to the suburbs I observed two or three mosques most highly ornamented, and from a brilliancy of colour and elegance of form by far the most attractive of any building I had yet beheld in these wild places; but though it was getting dark when I entered the town ... it was at once easy to perceive that Tirana was as wretched and disgusting as its fellow city [i.e. Elbasan], save only that it excelled in religious architecture and spacious market places."

More than eighty years later in the early 1930s, Dayrell Oakley-Hill (1898-1985), a retired British officer arrived in Albania to help organise its Gendarmerie. On arrival in Tirana, he found:

"... the town centre was a large open space, with the isolated white parliament house on the right as you approached. Opposite, on the east side, was the clock tower and the handsome mosque of Suleiman Bey ..."

Writing his memoirs (*An Englishman in Albania*) many years later in the 1950s, Oakley-Hill remarked;

"Tower and mosque are still there, but that is about all."

In 1964, the French explorer, writer, and film-maker Albert Mahuzier (1907-1980) drove through Albania. In his book *L'Albanie entrouvre ses frontiers*, he described Tirana as, "... the capital without motor cars". And, that is how I found the city when I visited it in 1984. Thirty-two years later in 2016, the open space in the city's centre, the mosque, and the clock tower still stand, but much else has changed. No longer does it feel 'provincial' and off the beaten track. Full of traffic, Tirana has become a lively modern city without losing touch with its history. This is where my narrative begins.

Friday, 20th May 2016. Our British Airways flight from London landed in the rain, ahead of schedule, at Tirana's Mother Teresa International Airport near the village of Rinas. Saint Teresa of Calcutta (1910-1997), is the world's best-known person of Albanian parentage. Although she was born in Skopje, which is not within the borders of present day Albania, she is highly venerated by many Albanians. While engaging a taxi at the airport, we learnt that Albania uses two currencies interchangeably – its own, the 'Lek', and the Euro.

Our yellow Mercedes taxi pulled up outside the small Star Hotel in the Rruga I Dibrës. It is dwarfed by its neighbour, the multi-storey, luxurious Hotel Tirana International that looms over the beautiful wide open expanse of Skanderbeg Square in the city's centre. The tall hotel was built in the late 1970s, and was then named "Hotel Tirana". It was where our tour group was put up in 1984. Then, the Hotel Tirana was the only tall building in the city. Now, other 'skyscrapers' are being built.

Our small room had windows looking out towards Skanderbeg Square. The room (and most of the others that we were to stay in) came equipped with two pairs of rubber sandals ('flip-flops'). These were necessary because our bathroom was essentially what trendy designers describe as a 'wet room'. Similar sandals were provided in all the hotel rooms in which I stayed in 1984.

The two-storey Star was in a building that pre-dated WW2. In the corridor leading to the bedrooms, there were two glass-fronted bookshelves. Their shelves were filled with old books. It was not the usual lightweight holiday reading-matter that is often found discarded by hotel guests. Instead, there was a collection of old, well-worn books, mostly hardbacks, all printed in Russian. Some of them were Russian translations of classics such as novels by Victor Hugo and Jules Verne, but most of them were by Russian authors. We asked the receptionist about them. He told us that the books belonged to the owner of the hotel, an Albanian. That was all he knew.

Albania severed relations with its benefactor and mentor, the USSR, in 1961. Cordial relations with Russia began to deteriorate in 1955, when Nikita Khrushchev began nurturing friendship between his country and Yugoslavia. The latter had been Albania's ally briefly (helping the

Communist partisans in WW2), but became its enemy in 1948 when the Yugoslav leader Josip Broz Tito broke with Russia's Stalin. Under Enver Hoxha's leadership, Albania not only broke with its larger Balkan neighbour and the enormous USSR, but also with the Peoples' Republic of China. It had been on warm comradely terms with China from the late 1950s until soon after Mao Tse Tung's death in 1976. The owner of the hotel's library of Russian books must have had a good command of the Russian language, as well as access to a supply of Soviet publications. It was likely that these books were acquired before the Albanian-Soviet split.

At the café beneath the hotel, we were served by a friendly young man, who spoke a few words of English, and later greeted us whenever we walked past or entered the café. I had expected to find Turkish coffee served all over Albania, but although we were offered this occasionally, Italian-style coffee predominated. Throughout Albania, we were served excellent espresso coffees. Whether it was espresso or Turkish, coffee was always served with a glass of water. This was always, *uje cesme* (piped water, i.e. tap water). We were advised in a few restaurants to order bottled-water, but we usually drank tap water, and it did us no harm.

Skanderbeg Square is a vast open space with expansive lawns and surrounded by public buildings. It feels satisfyingly spacious. Looking eastwards beyond the eighteenth century highly decorated Et'hem Bey Mosque and the tall free-standing clock-tower next to it, the mountains embracing Tirana make an attractive backdrop. Like Trafalgar Square in London, Skanderbeg Square is unique. It could not be mistaken for any other square in Europe, and more than anything else in the city it gives Tirana its defining identity. In the centre of the square there is an imposing equestrian statue depicting Albania's national hero George Kastrioti, who is best known as 'Skanderbeg'. We walked inside the colonnade (facing the square) that forms the front of the former Palace of Culture. Its construction was begun by the Soviets, and abandoned by them when Enver Hoxha divorced Albania from the USSR. It was completed by the Chinese. Today, the building houses the Opera House, various commercial offices, the National Library, a couple of cafés, a tourist office, and a wonderful bookshop, Librari Adrion.

The Et'hem Bey Mosque, which both Lear and Oakley-Hill described, stands near the former Palace of Culture. It is covered with frescoes, both on its external and its internal walls. Some of them are figurative, depicting trees, plants, mosques, landscapes, and towns such as Istanbul. This makes them unusual because figurative images like these are rarely found decorating mosques. Outside the western Balkans, if they are decorated at all, mosques are commonly decorated with abstract patterns and calligraphy, and occasionally floral and plant motifs. The frescoes in Et'hem Bey were painted in a florid, almost rococo, Italianate style by an artist who trained in Venice. Several men were praying on the lovely patterned carpets that lined the floors of the interior of the mosque and in the glassed-in veranda attached to it. A curtain at the side of the main entrance covered the entrance to a room reserved for women worshippers. Lopa was welcomed into the main mosque (which is normally forbidden to women), and so could view the frescos.

Much of Albania's population is nominally Muslim. When Lear visited Albania in 1848, he recorded that all women *whatever* their religion hid their faces in public. In contrast, during the three weeks that we were in Albania, we saw no more than a handful of women wearing head coverings. Wherever we went, Albanians of all religious persuasions were keen to assure us that there always was, and still is, inter-religious harmony in their country.

We walked from the mosque to the elegantly simple red brick National Bank of Albania (also facing the square). It was built by the Italians before WW2. The recently built Orthodox Cathedral stands close by, but away from the square. Its not particularly attractive exterior belies the beauty of its interior. Many of the wrought metalwork votive candle holders were decorated with double-headed eagles. These were the double-headed eagles of Byzantium, similar to those of Skanderbeg, which appear on Albania's national flag. The interior of the cathedral was airy and circular, with a modern iconostasis. Opposite the Cathedral, we saw a building that is about to become a 'museum of surveillance'. This activity was important during the Communist era, when at least 20% of the population worked for the Sigurimi (the secret police), spying on their workmates, neighbours, and even members of their family. It was not yet open while we were in Albania.

After eating a snack in the lively pedestrianised Shtetitoria (promenade) Murat Toptani that runs beside the last remains of the walls of Tirana's castle, which was built in Byzantine times (before 1300 AD), we entered the Tirana International Hotel to meet our friend Bujar (not his real name). For years after visiting Albania in 1984, I held a mental image of the appearance of the foyer of this hotel. On entering it in 2016, it was much as I remembered. There were still only two lifts to the upper floors. These and the reception desk were exactly where they had been in 1984. We sat waiting for our friend in armchairs located in the very place where members of the Sigurimi dressed in smart suits used to lounge (in armchairs) in 1984, keeping an eye on affairs in the hotel.

After drinking coffee with Bujar in the hotel's elegant ground floor bar – a popular meeting place for 'those who matter', we crossed the corner of Skanderbeg Square to await the opening of the ticket counter of the Opera, which is in the former Palace of Culture. This counter is only open for a couple of hours each day. We bought tickets for that evening's performance of *I Montecchi e Capuletti*, an opera by the Italian composer Bellini.

Tirana Opera house foyer: Sea shells used as musical instruments

The foyer of the opera house was plain, devoid of furniture except for several glass-topped cases displaying a selection of traditional Albanian folk-music instruments, including some sea-shells. We sat down in the old-fashioned auditorium. The seats were aged, a bit rickety, but comfortable. They reminded me of the seats in some of the now mostly demolished older cinemas in Bangalore (India). The opera was superbly performed – good singing (in Italian), good acting, and wonderful music. The scenery was simple but effective. Throughout the show, people filmed scenes from the opera on their mobile telephones despite earlier exhortations (both in Albanian and English) to switch them off. Apart from the unauthorised filming, the audience was quiet, appreciative, and generous with applause, which was well-deserved. Quite by chance, we were sitting next to a lady from England, an English nun living in Albania. Her mission was caring for Albanian girls, who had been repatriated after having been 'trafficked' and misused. Since the end of Communism, many well-meaning foreigners like her have come to Albania to assist with its 'problems'.

The opera performance ended at about 11pm. The dining room of the Tirana International Hotel was still open. We were given good service in its stylish second floor terrace restaurant, but the food quality was unremarkable compared with what we ate in Albania subsequently. Many years earlier in 1984, I ate in this restaurant. Then, our tour group was fed, isolated and out of sight of other (i.e. Albanian) diners. Wherever we ate in Albania in '84, we were isolated from Albanians. There were at least two reasons for this. One was to reduce the risk of us communicating with Albanians. The other was to prevent the Albanians from seeing the good food we were being served. For, in 1984 food shortages in Albania were dire. Blendi Fevziu wrote in his biography of the dictator, *Enver Hoxha: The Iron Fist of Albania*, that in 1984 that Albanians had: "... an average per capita income of 15 US dollars a month...", and subsisted on "... meagre food rations. In some towns, a family of four would get no more than one kilogram of meat per month..." To add to their hardships, people were forbidden from raising animals or growing crops for their own use. I was unaware of this in '84.

New Tirana: a bell tower of the Orthodox Cathedral and a new skyscraper behind it

Horses and a mini tractor on Mount Dajti

Saturday, 21st May 2016 Distant church bells and bright sunlight woke us early. We walked away from Skanderbeg Square along the Rruga i Dibrës, where we saw several buildings, typically Balkan in design, dating back to well before WW2. The narrow Rruga Kostandin Kristoforidhi, which was named in honour of a man who was born in Elbasan in 1827 (a writer, a translator of the Bible into Albanian, and involved in Albania's struggle for independence), led us to even smaller lanes. They ran between old walls punctuated occasionally by carved wooden doors. The walls protected the privacy of families living within them. These dwellings from the Ottoman (pre-1912) era were typical of those I have seen elsewhere in the Balkans. They hark back to the harem mentality that prevented strangers' eyes from seeing the family's womenfolk. Tiled roofs and treetops were all that could be seen above the walls. At one house, where the street doors were open, a woman sweeping her yard let us peek into her flower-filled luxuriant garden. This charming enclave of 'old Tirana' was overlooked by high-rise buildings, some recent and others dating back to Communist times. We had seen part of what Oakley-Hill saw in the early 1930s:

"… the old town; a tangled area of shops and handicraft workshops, a fair number of private houses…"

Further along Rruga Kostandin Kristoforidhi, we passed the backs of three large apartment blocks that were built in the Communist era. Compared with many of the blocks of flats that were built in Hoxha's time, these looked superior in quality. Many of the shops and restaurants at street level had cages containing little birds, which chirped continuously. Caged-birds are very popular all over Albania. I cannot remember seeing them in 1984.

Near Skanderbeg Square, we passed the remains of an Ottoman *turbe* (an enclosure housing the grave of a notable Muslim), and then reached a sculptural monument. Designed in the socialist-realism style, it commemorated the partisans (Communist) of Tirana, who fought between the 28th of October and the 17th of November 1944. Enver Hoxha and his forces timed their triumphal arrival in the capital carefully, entering it on the 28th November to coincide with the (32nd) anniversary of Albania's independence. A fair was being held near to the monument. Turkish food was on sale to raise money for financially disadvantaged Albanian students.

The southern end of Skanderbeg Square is funnel-shaped in plan. The funnel's sides are formed by elegant, three-storey governmental buildings, whose windows have green-painted wooden shutters. These were built by the Italians in the 1930s. Along with the square, they were part of a design to modernise Tirana in line with the grandiose town-planning that appealed to fascist (and other) dictators. This pre-war town-planning enhances the wide-open, uncrowded feeling of the city's centre. The straight Bulevardi Dëshmorët I Kombit (Boulevard of National Heroes) descends gently from these buildings to the University of Tirana, an example of Italian Fascist architecture which reminded me of buildings constructed in Rome's EUR district (built to commemorate 20 years of fascism in Italy). Designed in the last two years of his life by the Italian architect Gherardo Bosio (1903-1941), it was originally the Casa del Fascio (House of Fascism).

When Mahuzier was in Tirana in 1964, he said that the Boulevard, which was then named 'New Albania', resembled the Champs Elysées without any traffic at all. This has changed. Though not quite as busy as its

French counterpart this main axis of the capital carries plenty of traffic. We walked along the boulevard past the Museum of Modern art, in whose garden workmen were busy assembling an installation by the Japanese artist/architect Sou Fujimoto (see later).

Next to the museum, we looked over a fence at what was once Tirana's classiest hotel, the Dajti. Designed by Italian architects (Gherardo Bosio and Gio Ponti), built in 1939, and opened shortly afterwards, this is where most foreign visitors were put up before the opening of the Hotel Tirana (now Tirana International). When I visited Tirana in 1984, the Dajti was reserved for VIP foreign guests. Today, the place is uninhabitable, on the verge of collapse. It has not been demolished because there are plans to restore it. On one wall of the hotel, I saw some graffiti scrawled in English: "There is no good system except a sound system". While I was taking photographs of the dilapidated hotel, we met two British tourists of Pakistani origin, who live in London. They told us that they were visiting Albania to challenge what they referred to as "the negative stereotypical views" of the region, which they feel were held by many people in the UK.

Before beginning our walk along the Boulevard, we had visited the ageing National Theatre. A Pirandello play (*Play without a Script*) was to be performed in Albanian that evening. The charming ladies clustered around the ticket desk assured us that we would enjoy it because it was going to be full of song and dance. We bought a couple of tickets. The theatre was near a building, which was undergoing serious repairs. It had windows and doors with arabesque arches, which reminded me of the Doge's Place in Venice. Like so many edifices near Skanderbeg Square, it was built by the Italians in the early 1930s, and used to be Tirana's branch of the Italian insurance company Assicurazioni Generali di Trieste e Venezia.

Opposite the 'Generali' building, we spotted a hemispherical (dome-shaped) concrete bunker typical of those which Enver Hoxha placed all over the country to counter invading armies. Surrounded by building materials, I thought that it was a left-over from the era of dictatorship, but it was not. It had been built recently by the current socialist government as a memorial to the past. Its presence annoyed many of Tirana's citizens, who preferred not to be reminded of Albania's grim history. It has been a target for vandals.

The southern side of the Hotel Dajti overlooks Tirana's river, the Lana. Confined between neatly manicured parallel sloping grassy banks, the fast-flowing stream looks more like a canal than a river. After crossing it, the boulevard passes two memorials relating to the Communist era. The older of these is the impressive but ugly Pyramid. Covered in graffiti and looking distinctly tatty, this gigantic glass and concrete pyramid was constructed soon after Enver Hoxha's death in 1985. It is nearly as tall as its neighbour, the multi-storey Raffeisen Bank tower block. When it was first opened, the Pyramid served as a mausoleum containing mementoes of the deceased dictator. After Communism ended in 1990, it fell into disrepair, and was vandalised. Parts of it are now used for occasional exhibitions. We watched streams of intrepid people crawling up its sloping concrete supports towards its apex. Near to it, there is a newer monument in the form of a pedestrian bridge that passes beneath a large bell. It commemorates the victims of Hoxha's reign of terror. Alongside that, a perforated concrete wall serves as a reminder of the terrible disturbances, a civil war, that occurred in 1997. These troubles followed the collapse of government sanctioned 'Pyramid schemes', which were massive financial swindles. Many financially naïve Albanians were persuaded to invest large amounts of money, sometimes their entire fortunes, in saving schemes which gave the promise of unbelievably high returns. When they inevitably collapsed, many Albanians were left impoverished. There were plenty of losers, and only a handful of unscrupulous winners.

Almost opposite the Pyramid but across the Boulevard from it, there is a park which was formerly part of the 'Bllok'. This was an enclave - rather like Beijing's Forbidden City - where only the senior members of the Communist Government of Albania lived - in luxury, hidden from of the eyes of ordinary citizens. Although life in the Bllok was more comfortable than elsewhere in Albania, it was precarious. At the 'drop of a hat', people in the Bllok could fall out of favour with Enver Hoxha, and then were forced to face hardships in prison camps if they were not exterminated.

Albanians were forbidden entry to the Bllok unless they had specific work to do there. Today, this area is one of the most fashionable parts of Tirana. It contains many new buildings but also once elegant apartment buildings that date back to the Communist era and before. The creation of a 'reservation' for senior Communist officials dated back to before 1945 when Oakley-Hill (see above) visited Tirana as part of an UNRRA relief mission. He recalled that in those early days of Communist control, part of what was to become the Bllok was already fenced off and guarded securely by troops because the Party and Government leaders were living there in some of Tirana's then best housing.

At the edge of the park next to the Boulevard, there stands a large governmental building, the Zyrat e Parlamentit (Parliament Office). It was built by the Italians before WW2. The Post-Block Memorial stands close by. This includes three reminders of dictatorship: a short section of the Berlin wall (donated by the City of Berlin); a well-restored hemispherical concrete bunker; and four concrete mine props. The bunker was that which guarded the main entrance to the Bllok. The props were part of the mining complex at Spac, a concentration camp where many of Hoxha's opponents were forced to do unpaid hard labour. The Berlin Wall fragment signified enforced separation from the outside world. I noticed a couple of neglected disused, graffiti-covered bunkers elsewhere in the park, part of the Bllok's defensive ring. They were covered with graffiti. A statue of Ismail Qemal Vlora, the founding father of modern Albania and its first Prime Minister, stands on the Boulevard between the Memorial and the Presidential Palace.

We ate a good lunch in the Bllok at the King House Restaurant on Rruga Ibrahim Rugova, near the former home of Enver Hoxha. Shemsi, the brother of a London friend, who inspired me to write my first book about Albania, arrived in his Mercedes. He offered to take us to see Mount Dajti, the 1600 metre mountain east of Tirana. We had thought that he would drive us to the cable car that whisks people up the mountain in about fifteen minutes, but he had another plan.

The road up to Dajti climbed through Tirana's hilly eastern suburbs before entering open countryside. Away from town, it became a steep winding mountain lane whose surface had deteriorated badly. Considering that we were so close to the capital, I was surprised by the appalling state of the road to one of Tirana's major excursion sites. It was narrow, curvy, rich in pot-holes, poor in tarmac, and had numerous tight hairpin bends. Shemsi drove us skilfully upwards along a road that became more awful the higher we climbed. On the way, we passed one or two mildewed concrete bunkers that were placed many decades ago to defend various sensitive military installations and mountain retreats that were reserved for Enver Hoxha's *nomenklatura*.

Oakley-Hill wrote that in the 1930s:

"If one could not go far afield, there was the plateau on Mount Dajti. After the olive groves and the foothills, the track zig-zagged steeply up the rocks, and one came out on to the wide grassy plateau with woods beyond ... The place was so numinous that I positively expected things to happen, a dance of dryads, even the pipes of Pan..."

Eventually, we emerged from the forest and parked near some grassy meadows just beneath Dajti's summit. It was almost as Oakley-Hill described, but not quite as magical. Next to our parking place, we saw men trying to hire their ponies and horses to visitors, who had braved the mountain on this grey afternoon. Some of these animals galloped, riderless, hither and thither across the meadows. I heard no pipes of Pan, nor saw any dryads. Instead, I saw some young men buzzing around the plateau in miniature tractors. There were also a few men trying to encourage visitors to test their skills with guns by firing them at balloons.

We entered a hotel that resembled an airport control tower, and served as the upper station of the cable-car. We took a lift to the bar in the circular observation post at the top of the building. The seating area rotated, offering splendid views of the mountains around us and Tirana spread out far beneath us. Outside the hotel, we walked along a windswept terrace that afforded brilliant views of the city. Even though the weather was bad, we could see the port of Durrës on the Adriatic Sea, almost fifty kilometres from where we were standing. Using my telephoto lens, I could see silhouettes of tall buildings in Durrës as well as cranes on its harbour jetty. Shemsi drove us back down the appalling road that we had ascended earlier. Little did I realise then that I would have to try to replicate his careful driving technique often during the coming days when we drove around Albania in our hired car.

Just before the entering the National Theatre, we heard the muezzin's call to prayer being broadcast from loudspeakers high up on the minaret of the Et'hem Bey Mosque. The ensemble of buildings including the mosque and its neighbouring clock tower, the former Palace of culture, the National Museum, and the Italian-built buildings, contributes to the special feeling that Skanderbeg Square evokes in me. It might not have the grandeur of, for example, Place Vendome or Piazza San Marco, but it has a dignity that befits the hero after whom it is named.

The rectangular auditorium of the National Theatre was delightfully old-fashioned, with many drapes and an upper gallery that extended around three sides of it. Everything was red including the plush upholstery of the comfortable seats. Although we did not understand much of it, the Pirandello play was acted beautifully. The expressive acting was so good that we could get a fair idea of what was going on. It compensated for our inability to understand the words. If the actions of actors move me more than their words, I feel this is a sign of truly skilful acting. As the great actor Constantin Stanislavski said: "The language of the body is the key that can unlock the soul". This is exactly what the actors in Tirana achieved.

After the play was over, we ate at a restaurant, owned by a Greek woman, on the pedestrianised Murat Toptani Promenade. Toptani (1867-1918) was an Albanian born in the Ottoman Caucasus. He was an artist, poet, and one of the signatories of the Albanian Declaration of Independence in 1912. One dish we enjoyed contained chicken with rice, mushrooms, champagne, and four cheeses (gouda, kaçkavalli, parmesan, and mozzarella).

Walking back to the hotel, we passed the *turbe*, which was illuminated, and then we stumbled across a simple monument (put up in 2016). It was a plaque written both in Albanian and Hungarian, commemorating the Hungarian Janos Hunyadi (1407-1456), a contemporary of Skanderbeg (1405-1468). Both men were formidable opponents of the Ottoman armies. Hunyadi delayed the Turkish conquest of Hungary by sixty years, and Skanderbeg's activities prevented the Turks from invading Italy. It had been an ambition of the Turkish Sultan Mehmed II ('The Conqueror'; 1432-1481) to kennel his dogs in St Peter's in Rome, but Skanderbeg's resistance to his armies in Albania helped thwart him. Both the Hungarian and the Albanian were given the rarely awarded title of 'Athleta Christi' (Champion of Christ) by various popes during the fifteenth century. Before retiring to our hotel, we admired the floodlit Mosque of Et'hem Bey, and its neighbour the clock-tower that was built in 1822 and made taller in 1928.

*Folk musicians with a statue of Skanderbeg behind them.
The tall building on the right is the Hotel Tirana International*

Children sketching on Skanderbeg Square. In the foreground, a depiction of the Et' hem Bey Mosque

Folk dancers in Skanderbeg Square.

Sunday, 22nd May 2016 Our friend Shemsi met us at our hotel, and then drove us to a suburb close to the centre of Tirana to sample a traditional Albanian breakfast. He took us to a restaurant, which had no name on its facade. We were its youngest customers that morning. The centrepiece of the breakfast was *paçe* soup (known as '*khash*' in Armenian, and '*pache*' in Persian). Cooked with just about every part of an animal, in our case veal, it had a slightly gelatinous texture and tasted delicious. It was served with pilaf (a rice and meat dish), bowls of condiments (including red chilli grains and sliced garlic marinated in vinegar), bread, and thick yoghurt. We washed this feast down with glasses of wine and raki. Albanian raki, which is made from fruit (not grain), is different to the aniseed flavoured Turkish raki. It has some resemblance to Italian Grappa and some Yugoslav hard spirits.

After this filling breakfast, Shemsi drove us through Tirana to the Rruga Elbasanit (it leads towards Elbasan). That sunny Sunday morning the road was busy with many vehicles and crowds of pedestrians. We entered a modern café-cum-patisserie called Lej & Laj - it described itself as a 'bakery shop' - and just managed to find a small table on its crowded terrace. We enjoyed espresso coffee and fresh baklava dripping with honey. Outside the patisserie, there were people at the curb side selling all kinds of farm produce: herbs, fruit, honey, alcohol and yogurt. These were packed in re-cycled soft-drinks bottles, and plastic containers. Shemsi explained that these country people visited Tirana to sell their wares to passers-by. Seeing them reminded me of something that I observed when wandering alone around Tirana in 1984. I spotted two ladies lurking in a side street, who were selling small bunches of leaves, maybe herbs. They were extremely suspicious of my attention, because any form of private enterprise in Albania was illegal in 1984.

As he drove us to Skanderbeg Square, we asked Shemsi why many of the older buildings in Tirana had exposed concrete beams and bare unfinished, uneven brickwork, rather than plaster on their exteriors. He said that it was cheaper not to put plaster on the outsides of buildings. That made sense, but it also made for an unfinished look. Having said that, many buildings in the UK have un-plastered brickwork exteriors, but the brickwork is neatly, evenly, and often decoratively finished, quite unlike what we saw in Albania.

There was no motor traffic in Skanderbeg Square that Sunday. Instead, there were many cyclists and pedestrians on the streets surrounding it. Under the colonnade of the former Palace of Culture, we saw youngsters with drawing boards, sketching. Many were making competent pictures of the mosque. The children were friendly, and thrilled to be photographed as they worked on their pictures. Some adults with clipboards explained to us that the square had been rendered free of traffic as a trial in advance of carrying out proposed plans to change the layout of the square, possibly making it permanently traffic-free.

At the south end of the square, a troupe of folk musicians and dancers, dressed in colourful folk costumes, was performing traditional Albanian songs and dances on a makeshift stage. We joined the appreciative audience that included lots of small children, who danced on the pavement alongside the stage. All around the square, cyclists were 'making a day of it'. Family groups were having fun in small pedal-driven cars that were available for hire.

At the nearby National Art Gallery, we viewed its superb collection of socialist-realism paintings and sculptures. I am glad that these have been preserved despite the radical political changes that have occurred since they were crafted. Although the sentiments that they express may be outdated, the artworks were well-executed. Many of them portrayed an optimistic view of the brave new world that Hoxha's Marxism-Leninism hoped to create.

The gallery was also hosting a fascinating temporary exhibition: a huge collection of posters advertising Albanian films made in the country during the Communist era. As works of art, these vivid posters were satisfying. However, the informative bilingual (Albanian and English) captions explained that there was more in these posters than met the eye. An example of this was the poster for the film *Skettere 43*, which was first shown in 1980. In the following year, Enver Hoxha's close associate, the Prime Minister of Albania Mehmet Shehu, died suddenly in mysterious circumstances. That year, 1981, the film was forbidden for public viewing because its screenwriter was the discredited former Prime Minister's son, Baskim Shehu. The poster made for this film was never displayed again because it carried Baskim's name. Baskim languished in prison from 1981 until the fall of Communism in 1990. Another poster, that made for the film *Intendenti*, was initially withdrawn and its artist taken in for questioning because he had depicted the sun in white instead of the officially favoured colour red. Both the artist and his poster escaped punishment. There were a few posters with Russian script. These dated back to the era when the USSR was giving assistance to Albania. At least one of these early films was an Albanian-Soviet co-production. This was the 1954 film *Skenderbeu*, about Skanderbeg, which was acted by both Albanian and Russian actors.

We walked into the Bllok to view the large, unremarkable, rambling house in which Enver Hoxha lived with his family. It stands in a corner plot on Rruga Ibrahim Rugova. Although it was the residence of an extremely powerful head of state, it lacked both glamour and elegance. Set well back from the road in gardens that were not well-maintained, this undistinguished mansion would not have looked out of place in an Outer-London suburb, maybe in Bromley or Edgware. Across the road on another corner plot, is the former home of Mehmet Shehu. It was a more elegant house than Enver's.

The park containing the Post Bllok Memorial backs onto a side road that gives cars access to Shehu's former home. We spoke to a security guard at its the main entrance, who explained in good English that Hoxha's former home is larger than Shehu's. Both are used to accommodate occasional important visitors and to host special meetings. The most important guests get accommodated in Hoxha's old residence.

Leaving the Bllok, we walked towards the river, and crossed it close to the new, unremarkable Roman Catholic Cathedral. On our way, we passed various government buildings dating back to the Communist era. Outside one of them, there was a sign made with huge plastic letters that read "KORRUPSJION" (i.e. 'corruption'), and beneath it in smaller letters "www.stopkorrupsionit.al". We were told by many people that corruption plagues modern Albania. Back in London, I looked at this website. Set up by a government department, anyone can use it to report (anonymously or not) irregularities in the provision of services, both public and private.

Near the cathedral, we saw an attractive old stone bridge with two unequally sized arches. Like a folly in an English country house garden, it straddled a grassy space. We had arrived at the Ura e Tabakëve (the Tanners' Bridge), which was built in the eighteenth century to span the river, whose course has long since been diverted. It used to carry a major road that connected Tirana with Debar far to the east of it (now in Macedonia). Today, it is a tourist attraction. From there, we strolled back to our hotel, passing along the Rruga Presidenti George W Bush, named after the first US President ever to visit Albania (in 2007). Albania has a long-standing connection with America. Until 1944, when Enver Hoxha assumed power, many Albanians emigrated to the USA. After 1990, Albania resumed friendly relations.

After resting in our air-conditioned room, we went to the National Museum. Bujar had invited us to the official opening of an exhibition of photographs by a photographer from the People's Republic of China, Zeng Yi. Several dignitaries gave speeches in Albanian, which were translated into Mandarin for the Chinese photographer by a short, elderly, balding Albanian man. Throughout the opening ceremony another Chinese photographer darted about the assembled guests, taking pictures with his camera that bore a huge lens, like the barrel of an artillery piece. After the speeches, we looked at the pictures in the exhibition, mostly black and white, and all beautifully executed.

I asked Bujar about the interpreter. He told me that he must have learnt Mandarin back in the days before the late 1970s when Albania and China were bosom pals. Enver Hoxha kept up the appearance that all was well with China until the very last moment. Hardly anyone in Albania knew in advance that the two countries were about to part company. At the time of the split, Bujar was working in a small country place. It was during the period that intellectuals were sent out to remote country places to work alongside the 'peasants', just as happened in China during its Cultural Revolution. One day at noon, the public loudspeakers were suddenly switched on, and Radio Tirana announced that China had become Albania's deadly enemy. Up to that moment, most Albanians had believed that China was Albania's closest friend and ally.

Some years before our visit to Albania, I met a retired Indian diplomat who had been stationed in Beijing at the time of the rift. He told me that he had read a copy of the open letter that Hoxha had addressed to the Chinese, and marvelled that such a tiny country as Albania had had the nerve to treat a country as powerful as China with so much contempt. The letter ended with the words:

"The Chinese leadership will fail in its intrigues. The reactionary act it committed against Albania is revolting... Our cause is just! Socialist Albania will triumph!"

I reminded the Indian that it was not the first time Hoxha had done this. He had already told Yugoslavia's Tito, and then later the USSR's Khrushchev, to put it crudely, where to 'get off,' and to leave Albania to do its 'own thing'.

One of the guests at the opening was the wife of an Albanian diplomat, who had been stationed in China during the years of friendship. She told us that Chinese newspapers at that time were full of material about Albania. One day in China, she had heard one of her Chinese acquaintances saying that because there was so much about Albania in the Chinese press, it must have been a large country. This led to another Chinese person asking how large was Albania. Someone replied that he did not know exactly, but it must surely have been much bigger than China.

As we left the gathering at the museum, we said goodbye to the Chinese delegation. Although none of them seemed to be able to speak English, they gave us handshakes and warm smiles.

We returned to Skanderbeg Square, which was still free of motor traffic but full of cyclists. As the sun set over Tirana and the buildings surrounding square were bathed in its final rays, a jazz ensemble began playing where earlier we had watched the folk musicians and dancers. At one point, the call of the muezzin competed with the music.

After dinner, we watched old black and white film that was being projected in the open-air on a screen set up close to the attractively illuminated gold-coloured Monumenti i 100 vjetorit të Pavarësisë (Monument to 100 years of Albania's Independence). Containing copies of the signatures of the men who signed the Declaration of Independence, it resembled an oversized deconstructed London telephone box. That evening, screens had also been set up in the pedestrianised Toptani Promenade. A range of short films, mostly documentaries about wildlife, were being screened.

Enver Hoxha's home in Tirana's Bllok

Tirana, Krujë, Shkodër

Monday, 23rd May 2016 After breakfast out on the terrace of the café beneath the Star Hotel, we ordered a taxi. Before it arrived, we followed a sign next to the café that pointed the way to the Bahai centre. It turned out that this was right next door to the café. The centre has an attractive wrought iron gateway, and is housed in a pre-WW2 house. There were some Albanian Bahai adherents in the country as early as 1934, but not during the Hoxha years. Like so many other religious groups, the Bahai are re-establishing a foothold in post-Communist Albania.

Our taxi driver, whose English was adequate, was chatty. He was most happy about our enthusiasm for, and our curiosity about, his country. When he learnt that Lopa was from India, he wanted to know all about Kashmir. We told him what we could. Like so many Albanians, with whom we spoke, he was keen to emphasise that harmony between different religions reigned in his country. He was Muslim and married to an Orthodox Christian. Hearing that we were on our way to hiring a car to drive around Albania, he warned us that Albanian drivers are crazy, and we were not to hurry or do anything we did not feel was right however much other drivers hooted and yelled at us.

When we have hired cars in the past, we have been presented with a car which was almost new and flawless. This was not the case with Enterprise at Tirana's airport. We had ordered a Tata Indica car – I had chosen it because of the price and because I had not driven an Indian car since 1994, the first and only time that I have driven in India. Our Tata was distinctly tatty in appearance. It was covered in scratches and dents, all of which were carefully noted and photographed by the Enterprise representative and me. The upholstery was clean but looked well worn. He told us that the car was "quite new", and "…had only done about 32,000 kilometres". Dubious at first, I realised later that this unprepossessing looking vehicle was just the job for our trip.

I was pleased that we had not hired the car from an office in Tirana, where traffic was heavy, but instead from the airport, where traffic was light. Soon, we left the main Tirana to Shkodër 'highway', and then began winding our way uphill to the small town of Krujë, where Albania's hero Skanderbeg had his headquarters while he was combatting the Ottomans. In September 1848, Edward Lear made the same journey: "At two, we left the Skodra, or post road … and struck directly across the vale to Kroia – a winding ascent through green wooded hill-buttresses or shoulders, changed ere long for a sharp climb up to the foot of the great rock round which the town clusters and hangs…"

It took Lear two hours to reach Krujë. We took less than fifteen minutes.

Skanderbeg, Gjergj Kastrioti, the son of the noble-man Gjon Kastrioti, was taken by the Turks to Turkey as a young boy (as many Christian youths were in that time). He was (possibly forcibly) converted to Islam, educated as a soldier, and became a good fighter in the Ottoman Army. In 1443, aged thirty-eight, Skanderbeg along with several other Albanian soldiers deserted the Turks. He took command of the Castle at Krujë, from where he organised Albanian resistance against the Ottomans. After many military exploits, both in Albania and, also, in Italy (where he gave assistance to King Ferdinand I of Naples), Skanderbeg finally succumbed to malaria in 1468. This is a quick summary of the career of a man who saved Western Europe from becoming part of the Ottoman Empire. Albania did become part of the Empire, but in the words of a guidebook published in 1969 by Albturist, the state tourist agency of Albania:

"Although their heroic efforts were not crowned with final victory, the Albanian people did not kneel down. Throughout the centuries that followed, our people continued their resistance against the Ottoman feudal regime."

Just as Lear described over 160 years ago, the road became increasingly steep until we entered the town where level ground was a rarity. We parked the car on a sharply inclined street, and made our way to a café. Its terrace provided a great view of the town's castle, which overlooked us, and the old bazaar, which was several metres below us. We saw a few elderly people wearing traditional costumes, but everyone else was dressed in modern clothing.

We only had drinks in Krujë. Lear, whose visit and especially his imitations of the sounds made by steam locomotives enchanted Ali Bey of Krujë, was entertained to a meal that he found a challenge. After having accidentally upset a bowl of soup because he got a cramp in his leg whilst squatting on the floor, Ali Bey's English visitor was served:

"A pilaf of fowls, full of spices and bones, kebabs, a paste of rice, onions, and pie crust, and some round balls of chopped meat concluded the repast, some grapes excepted."

We stumbled along the shiny cobbles of the street that runs between the two lines of shops that make up the old bazaar. This has been extended since I saw it in 1984, but the extension has been made to look as if it were original. As in 1984, the shops in the bazaar were selling goods aimed at tourists: everything from tasteless 'tat' to some attractive antiques. One shop contained superb examples of traditional Albanian handicrafts, including some carved wooden cradles for babies and large antique embroidered cloths. Although the bazaar resembled what I remembered from my first visit, the town had become filled with new buildings, including mosques and churches. Many, but not all, of the old Ottoman era buildings, which made Krujë so attractive to me in 1984, have been demolished to make way for newer, mostly less-attractive, constructions. Nevertheless, Krujë, nestling in the wooded hills that surround it, was a lovely place to visit.

Leaving the cobbled market behind us, we began ascending the path to the castle complex. On our way, we passed an old stone structure that housed an outlet for a dried-up spring. It contained fragments of old carvings including an eight-pointed star, and just above the outlet for the water two carved animals facing each other. Nearby, two young boys selling small round green plums asked where we were from, and then tried selling us some of their fruit. Just before we reached the entrance to the castle, we met an elderly man sitting on a wall, selling books. He was their author. We greeted him, and said that we would look at his books after we had visited the castle.

Parts of the vast area inside the castle walls were still inhabited. Much of the space is covered with ruins of what had originally been Skanderbeg's castle and then later the Ottomans'. These ruins included a solitary watchtower and the base of a large minaret. We had read that there was a Bektashi mosque, the Dollma *Tekke* ('teqe' in Albanian. i.e. a Bektashi place of worship), in the grounds. A young man offered to guide us to it. Because the way to it was extremely rough and Lopa had a bad ankle, she decided to wait for me while I went to see the historic building. The young man explained to me (in good English) that he is a Bektashi, a member of a 'sect' of Islam (although many Muslims disclaim them) that is between Shia and Sufi. It has been long popular in Albania, Bulgaria, and Anatolia. Unemployed, as many Albanian graduates are, my guide spent his time looking after the *tekke* and its surroundings.

On our way to the shrine, we met a woman, aged about thirty, with her small child. She spoke some English, but mainly gossiped in Albanian with my new acquaintance. We were standing next to a heavily restored Ottoman *hammam* or bathhouse. Its bright new roof tiles detracted from its original beauty. After she left, my guide explained that when she had been orphaned, his family had informally adopted her and brought her up as if she had been their daughter. This was a kind thing to do in Albania at a time when food and fuel were in very short supply.

The eighteenth century *tekke* was well-preserved. Its interior walls and ceilings were covered with delicately painted frescos and lines of Arabic or Turkish calligraphy. I saw several tombs of dervishes (Sufi or Bektashi clerics) within the mosque, and others in its grounds. Near the *tekke*, I saw some old stone fragments that looked as if once they had been part of an earlier structure, maybe a church. My guide introduced me to an elder man who lived in a recently-built circular meeting hall next to the mosque. I was told that he had spent twelve years in prison during the Communist era simply because he was a Bektashi. Some years ago, I showed my friend Bejtulla Destani, an academic from Kosovo, the book by Albert Mahuzier, who visited Albania in the early 1960s before Enver Hoxha outlawed religion. It contained a photograph of a cleric in a *tekke* in Gjirokastër. As soon as he saw it, Bejtulla said that it was most likely that that such a man would have been killed by Hoxha's people soon after 1967.

The visit to the *tekke* took much longer than I had anticipated. As we were returning to where I had left Lopa, a security man came rushing towards me shouting: "Mister Adam?" I nodded, and he led me not to where I had left my wife, but instead to the Ethnographic Museum, where Lopa was becoming concerned that I might have been kidnapped or worse. After being reunited, I looked around the museum which was not only interesting because of its exhibits, but also because it was housed in a large old Ottoman residence.

Our path to the castle's exit led us past an impressive but incongruous fortress-like building. This was built in 1982 by the Communists as a shrine to honour Skanderbeg and to encourage patriotic sentiments. When we emerged from the castle, we stopped by the man selling books. He introduced himself as Professor Baki Dollma. He told us that he was related to the Dollma family after whom the *tekke* was named, and was a professor of history. Most of his books were in Albanian. We bought a volume about the history of Krujë that contained some English. When he learnt that I have written books, the author became very friendly, asked me to sit beside him, and then began addressing me as 'Professor'.

We left the professor, and returned to our car. I turned the ignition key. Nothing happened. I tried several times, and then assumed that we had rented a dud. I rang Enterprise. I was asked if I had used the remote control. I replied that I had not the remotest idea about it. I was told to look under the driver's seat where I would find a little box on a cable, and that I should always press the blue button on it before trying to start the car. It found it, and it worked. It would have been helpful to have known about this feature when we had taken possession of the vehicle at the airport.

We returned to the main road, and headed north towards Lezhë. Before reaching that town, we stopped at a roadside restaurant, Restaurant Juri (as in Yuri Gagarin), just south of Ishull Lezhë near a turning that led to the village of Tresh. We sat outdoors, and then ordered a plate of meatballs and another of sausages along with a serving of salad and some fried potatoes. Each of the meat dishes contained enough meat for two or three people. Delicious as it was, it seemed as if it would be a daunting task to finish it all.

The author with Professor Dollma (wearing hat) at Krujë.

Just as we were starting to eat, Juri appeared and placed a mound of liver and kidneys (sautéed with lemon rinds and green peppers) on the table, saying "Enjoy". Soon after this, he reappeared, and added a large plate of pickled vegetables to the enormous feast in front of us. Everything was delicious. It was not long before Juri was back again, this time to give us shot-glasses filled with fiery raki. We took sips of this, and before long Juri was pouring refills. I tried to object that I was driving. Juri shrugged his shoulders nonchalantly, and kept pouring. At many places in Albania we were given food that we had not ordered, told to try it, and then found it added to our bill. Juri only charged us for what we had ordered. The rest was 'on the house'. This meal and our time spent with Shemsi in Tirana helped us understand why Albanian hospitality is so highly rated by others who have visited the country.

In 1984, our tour group had been taken to see what was described as 'Mussolini's hunting lodge'. It was not 'Il Duce', but his son-in-law Count Ciano who built it (for his own use). I knew that it was somewhere near to Lezhë, but it was difficult to locate. We drove to the seaside resort of Shëngjin. This place, which used to be known by its Italian name San Giovanni di Medua ('Medua' for short), was once the port at which overseas visitors to Shkodër disembarked. One of these was Wadham

Peacock, who served as private secretary to the British Consul General in Shkodër between 1878 and 1880. In his book published in 1914, *Albania, The Foundling State of Europe*, he described landing at Medua. Coveted by the Serbians and the Montenegrins, this port was unimpressive by the standards of most other ports. Peacock wrote:

"… but the traveller who expects docks, or piers, wharves, warehouses and all the rest of the advantages of civilisation, will be disappointed…"

Because the sea was so shallow, passengers were transported in small boats from their steamers to the primitive rocky landing stage. These were:

"… manned by boatmen whose appearance was that of brigands, and whose looks and gestures were those of all of the ruffians of history and legend put together … In their belts were arsenals of weapons, pistols and long knives, and with eyes flashing they argued at the top of their voices in guttural Albanian over the passengers…"

Despite this: "But for all their savage appearance and quarrelsome manners the boatmen of San Giovanni di Medua were fine, honest fellows …"

Although no one we met during our trip to Albania looked as menacing as those boatmen, almost without exception everyone we met was fine and honest.

From Shëngjin, which has become a seaside resort popular with Albanians, we followed the shore line southwards along a road that ran between the sea and backwater lagoons. It was lined with tall Mediterranean pines, but we saw no sign of Ciano's lodge. We stopped to ask the way several times. Everyone knew what we were talking about, but were a bit vague as to where it was. Eventually, someone told us to head for the road between Ishull Lezhë and Vainn. Suddenly, I spotted a colourful old metal roadside sign bearing the words "Filiali Albturist, Hoteli Gjuetisi, Lezhe" ('gjuetise' means 'hunter'; Albturist was the Communists' state-run tourist company). We drove along the drive through a lush tree-filled garden, in which flowed a tributary of the nearby River Drin. An arched ornamental bridge crossed a stream clogged with weeds and bushes. It was partly hidden in amongst trees, which grow alongside it, and now stop it from collapsing. We parked outside a building that resembled what I saw in 1984, but it had become run-down. The Italian architects of this rambling building had made it look rustic by using irregularly-shaped roughly-hewn stones and timber logs. Creepers growing uncontrolledly (and unintentionally) on the walls and roofs added to the place's bucolic atmosphere.

The place seemed to be dead until, eventually, a waiter came out to meet us. He showed us the dining room and bar. They looked as if they had been left unchanged since the lodge was built. At first known as L'Albergo di Caccia (Italian for: Hunting lodge), this rustic-looking complex was constructed for Ciano in 1940, just after the Italians had invaded Albania. The waiter told us that there were rooms to rent, and unlocked one for us. The room looked comfortable but neglected, and had a damp musty smell. It might have been a peaceful place to stay, but rather spooky. We left this evocative spot and headed towards Lezhë.

The main road to Shkodër bypasses the centre of Lezhë, the town where Skanderbeg died. High above the River Drin that flows by Lezhë, we pulled into a petrol station. Its parking area overlooked the town, and provided an excellent view across the river of the ruined cathedral that contains the grave of Skanderbeg. The ruins are now protected from the elements by a pillared structure that was not present when I visited Lezhë in 1984. Looking upwards, we saw the walls of the town's ruined citadel crowning a hill behind the town.

It was late afternoon when we arrived at the Hotel Ambassador in the southern outskirts of Shkodër. Our hotel occupied the first and second floors of an unattractive modern block above some shops and offices. No one who worked in the hotel spoke any English, nor even much Italian. We coped, they coped. The first floor of the hotel was a bar-cum-restaurant. One of its customers translated for us. Our air-conditioned room was simple but comfortable. At first, I was a little dubious about the place, which looked characterless, but as our three night stay unfolded, we discovered that we were amongst very kind and hospitable people.

We drove into central Shkodër, and found that parking was difficult. We found a spot in a quiet back street, but some passers-by told us not to leave our car there because the city's police charged a lot for parking offences. We entered a parking-lot on the Rruga Ludovik Saraci. Its attendant was most fussy about exactly where and how we parked the car. We had to place it as close as possible to both the neighbouring vehicles and the boundary wall. The parking lot, which was a levelled building site (owned by a Protestant missionary organisation), was opposite the local quarters of the Order of the Knights of Malta (or 'Maltesers' as they were called in Albanian). It was a couple of minutes' walk from the

Pedonalja, the pedestrianised Rruga Kolë Idromeno, where people come to enjoy themselves.

When I visited Shkodër in 1984, what is now the Pedonalja was a lifeless street of well-preserved old buildings with a few closed shops with hardly anything displayed in their windows. Today, the historic buildings with their slatted upper storey wooden window-shutters are well-maintained, and the Pedonalja is a zone of joyous activity. In a way, the transformation of this street symbolised the transformation of Albania since the fall of Communism. Righteous sombreness has given way to joyful vibrancy.

Even in 1984, things in Shkodër were much better than in 1880 when the British barrister Edward Frederick Knight (1852-1925) paid it a visit during his Temple Chamber's Long Vacation. Writing in his *Albania: A narrative of recent travel*:

"Our first impressions of the city were not favourable. It had an appearance of melancholy decay, still trying to keep up an appearance ... there was a tea-garden-in-liquidation look about the place ... Everything had been allowed to fall into decay ... one rickety mosque was very funny; its steeple was tiled, if I may use the expression, with the sides of paraffin boxes and Huntley and Palmer's biscuit tins ... Every man we met – kilted Mussulman or white-clad Arnaut – was armed to the teeth ..."

None of this is applicable nowadays; the opposite is very much the case. Elsewhere in the town, Knight visited a grocery shop in the city, where he saw British exports including:

"... Huntley and Palmers biscuits, Cross and Blackwell's pickles, and, most wonderful of all, Brown Windsor soap, an article for which I should imagine that there could be no demand in Albania."

Well, I do not know about the soap, but can safely say there were a few foreigners living in Shkodër at the time (including the British Consul, his staff, and Paget – see below), who might have craved these British products.

The Pedonalja is lined with bars, cafés, and restaurants, as well as a good range of shops including a couple of well-stocked bookshops. People of all ages came to enjoy themselves on the Pedonalja in Shkodër. Cyclists wove their way skilfully between numerous merrymakers, shoppers, and outdoor café tables and chairs under colourful umbrellas advertising Albanian beers. Films were projected on outdoor screens. Occasionally, the call of the muezzin could be heard coming from the two minarets of the nearby Great Mosque. Gypsies begged for money, rather lackadaisically compared with others I have met elsewhere. We sat down outside a bar close to the new museum that exhibits photographs taken by the Marubi brothers, Italian-born photographers based in Shkodër in the early 20th century. According to a specialist in Albanian studies, Robert Elsie:

"Pietro Marubbi or Marubi (1834-1903) was an Italian painter and photographer who, as a supporter of Garibaldi, had emigrated from Piacenza, Italy, to Shkodra for political reasons around the year 1850."

We ordered sundowners. While I was enjoying my drink, a Facebook friend sent me a message, asking if we liked Italian food. I replied that we did, and he recommended a restaurant called "Pasta e Vino", which, he assured us, served very fine food. Before looking for it, we walked past the mosque, and reached Sheshi Demokracia (Democracy Square), the centre of the city. It is overlooked by the tall Hotel Rozafa, where I stayed in 1984. We entered its foyer, which looked somewhat dated, and asked the receptionist whether much had changed since 1984. She was too young to have known the hotel then, but explained that the layout of the ground-floor had been changed considerably. Across the square from the hotel stands the Migjeni Theatre, named in honour of a famous Albanian poet (see later), who was born in Shkodër.

It was a warm evening. We sat at an outside table at Pasta e Vino, and ate a good dinner, which included tortellini filled with ricotta and spinach served with cream and *spek*. After the meal, we chatted in Italian with the Albanian owner, who told us that he had worked in Italy and had a brother living in Modena. It turned out that his brother was my Facebook friend, who had recommended the restaurant without telling me his connection with it! After dinner, we drove back to our hotel, and enjoyed a late night raki in the bar.

Detail of an old spring outlet in Krujë. Note the eight-pointed Illyrian star pattern above the animals

In the old bazaar in Krujë

Count Ciano's hunting lodge near Lezhë

Mesi, Thethi, Shala, Koplik, and Shkodër

TUESDAY, 24th May 2016 On this grey day, we decided to venture into the northern Albanian mountains. The intrepid English explorer, anthropologist, artist, and promoter of Albanian political rights Edith Durham (1863-1944) wrote about them and their isolated inhabitants in her book, *High Albania*, published in 1909. It is still the best book written about this area.

We ate breakfast in the café of the Ambassador. From our table, we had a fine view of the Rozafa Fortress. Perched on the top of a mountain, it overlooks Shkodër, its lake, and the surrounding countryside. We noticed a greyish concrete monument close to our hotel. After breakfast, we crossed a grassy field, surrounded by oily car-repair workshops, to examine the four-sided structure. It was covered with pictures and texts in bas-relief. A pharmacist, whose shop was beneath the Ambassador Hotel, explained that this monument was erected to commemorate the immense amount of work that was done to repair the damage caused in the district around Shkodër after the huge earthquake that occurred in April 1979.

According to *Termeti I 15 Prillit 1979* (The Earthquake of April 15, 1979), a scholarly book published both in Albanian and English in Tirana in 1983, which I bought in Albania in 1984, this 'quake left 100,000 inhabitants homeless, of which 60,000 were in the District of Shkodër, and the rest in the District of Lezhë. There is a picture of the monument in the book that shows that its surroundings looked the same in the 1980s as they do now. Our hotel and the monument were in Bahçallëk, a suburb of Shkodër near where the River Drin (Drina i zi: Black Drin), which we could see and hear from our bedroom window, merges with the River Bojana (Buna) just before their combined waters drain into Lake Shkodër. Bahçallëk was particularly badly hit by the earthquake that also affected Montenegro and other parts of Yugoslavia badly. Enver Hoxha wrote of it:

"...There was a moment when the earth shook, the hills and mountains shook, many houses and villages were razed to the ground, but the Albanian was not shaken."

We drove to the Lead Mosque (Xhamia e Plumbit) that lies at the base of the mountain that is crowned by Rozafa Castle. The domes on this fine late eighteenth century mosque were reflected in the still waters of an inundated field. It had been locked up during Hoxha's times. Today, it is back in use but the original painted interior, which had become destroyed through years of neglect, has had to be replaced by something plainer. Before the earthquake of 1979, the Lead Mosque had been in the heart of the Tabak District of Shkodër. This area was completely razed by the 'quake and never rebuilt, so now the edifice stands alone surrounded by flat farmland and scattered dwellings.

We drove into Shkodër for some shopping (books, mainly) and coffee. Across a square facing the façade of the Franciscan Church, we found a big modern supermarket. Almost everything in it, except the fresh fruit and vegetables, was imported from Italy.

The sky became dark grey, the temperature dropped, and rain began falling heavily. We set off to find the bridge at Mesi. This was not simple because there were few if any road signs in the extensive, run-down industrial suburbs of Shkodër. We saw many dreary blocks of flats and ruined factories, one of which might well have been the copper wire factory that I almost visited in 1984, when we could not enter it because of a flash-flood.

We had bought a detailed map in Shkodër, but in the absence of road signs, this was of little use. Various people including a couple of policemen gave us vague or even misleading directions. Eventually, someone gave us useful instructions. We stopped in a petrol station during a heavy cloudburst, and checked whether we were on the right track; finally, we were. By now, the rain was pelting down. Almost accidentally, we found the turning that led to a rickety looking concrete road bridge across the fast-flowing River Kir, which drains water from the mountains of High Albania into the Drin i zi.

The concrete bridge is close to a beautiful Ottoman bridge built in the late eighteenth century. The old bridge has ten arches and is over one hundred metres long. We parked next to the new bridge, which was covered with vast puddles of water. Whenever a car passed us, it slowed down so that we were not splashed. This thoughtful behaviour is rare amongst drivers in London. The Ottoman structure did not collect puddles of water because it was gently humped, its roadway rising and falling over the curves of its arches. Even in the dreadful weather, its beauty shone through.

We followed the road, off which we had turned. It headed towards the high alpine village of Thethi. The rain fell relentlessly. We pulled in at a restaurant named Zalli I Kirit, outside of which there were many cars parked. I chose badly. One dish, fried kaçkavalli, proved that this cheese is best eaten uncooked. I ordered a hamburger. I was not expecting what arrived in front of me: a bun filled with salad, mayonnaise, and, instead of a burger, a few fried *qofte* (meatballs). People in the restaurant advised us not to drive further towards Thethi both because of the rain and, more importantly, because they felt that our vehicle was not robust enough.

We drove back into Shkodër's shabby rain-swept outskirts, and joined the main road that leads north to Han i Hotit on the Albanian side of the border with Montenegro. Near the turning for Koplik, we joined another road that was signposted to Thethi. We had been told that this would be better than the one we had abandoned after lunch. At first, the road ran across level agricultural terrain towards a wall of distant mountains. We passed a colourfully painted large hemispherical, dome-shaped, Hoxha-era concrete bunker. When I visited Albania in 1984, I remember seeing far more of these bunkers. Some areas of Albania looked as if they had been affected by a strange illness that caused the eruption of crops of oversized hemispherical concrete pimples. In 1984, one could not help noticing them. In 2016 they were less obvious, because many of them have become partly hidden by plants, destroyed, or damaged. Just beyond the bunker, a short distance north-east of Koplik i Sipërm, we passed a brand-new prison. Menacing-looking guards stood by the start of the short road that led to it. With its high walls, it seemed to be a very high security institution.

The narrow road headed straight for the steep, forbidding looking peaks, whose summits were lost in the grey storm clouds that had been gathering. Soon, the road began climbing and winding, following a valley between high mountains. Its surface varied continuously from acceptably smooth to incredibly rough. As we ascended, the scenery became increasingly grandiose. High above the forested slopes we caught glimpses of bare rocky crags dotted with patches of snow.

After having experienced first a hailstorm and then a thunderous downpour of rain, we reached a rusting sign punctured by shotgun bullets. It announced that we had arrived in Bogë, which is mentioned several times in Edith Durham's 1909 book as being a place inhabited by seventy-five feuding families. When Oakley-Hill (see above) was in Albania in the 1930s, the road from Shkodër to Bogë already existed. Beyond that, the going became tough even for experienced climbers like Oakley-Hill. Near the sign, but off the road, there were a few scattered houses and tiny fields. That was all. We continued ascending.

Beyond Bogë, the road surface suddenly improved. As snow began to fall, we followed this excellent stretch of road around numerous sharp hairpin bends until suddenly at the top of the valley, we reached a ridge. The new road ended abruptly. It became a rough track, which looked suitable only for hardy hikers and mules. A river of sharp black rock fragments varying in size disappeared into the clouds, and looked like a puncture repairer's paradise. There was a sign (in Albanian and English) that welcomed the traveller to 'Shala Commune', a district which also figures in Durham's book. We turned around on the narrow road, carefully avoiding putting our wheels over the edge of a fearful precipice that plunged down into a mist-covered void.

In 1922, another intrepid lady, the American novelist and political theorist, a colleague of the writer Ayn Rand, Rose Wilder Lane (1886-1968) wrote a book about her wanderings in the high mountains of northern Albania, *The Peaks of Shala*. It was while she was trekking through the remote Shala district that she contracted pneumonia, which she endured stoically. Had we been able to continue along this impossible looking track that is described on maps as "SH 21" (i.e. Rrugë Shtetërore 21 = State Road 21), we would have reached the isolated mountain commune of Thethi, which has recently become a popular tourist area. We returned down the valley. After passing a snow-covered marble monument recording a recent driving tragedy, we enjoyed an ever-changing series of stunning vistas with snow-covered greyish mountains dissolving in the clouds.

The weather improved when we reached the village of Zagorie, where we stopped for a coffee in a comfortably furnished modern café opposite a petrol station. Nearby, we saw a lovely church standing alone in the fields. Its exterior looked in good condition and its tiled roof looked new. Well over a century before we arrived there, this village was visited by Wadham Peacock (see above), who wrote:

"The little village of Zagora, in which I was spending a day or two, lies at the head of the long, wedge-shaped piece of stony land, running up from the lake and shut in by bare and lofty mountains, which constitutes the territory of the Skreli tribe … the tribe has winter pasturage near Medua…"

Peacock described a meal he had there:

"The usual mountaineer's supper was soon prepared – roast mutton and cakes drenched in honey, and then … coffee … and more cigarettes …"

We spotted a grisly memorial just west of the village on a slight rise by the side of the road. Two concrete posts supported a metal bar from which a wire hangman's noose dangled. The legend in Albanian on one of the monument's pillars read (in translation): "Be grateful and praise their work for the freedom of the motherland in 1918" On the other pillar, there was a short list of names, and the date 2013. Most of Albania was occupied by Austrian forces in 1916. The view from this monument was of low hills and high mountains beyond them in one direction, and, in the other, the distant waters of Lake Shkodër glinting in the afternoon sunshine. This was the land for which the patriotic Albanian martyrs, who were being commemorated, died.

As the weather had improved, we decided to try to drive down to the shore of the eastern side of Lake Shkodër. We drove through the town of Koplik towards the lake. At one point, we crossed a disused, weed-infested railway track. This used to carry freight between Albania and the former Yugoslavia. It was under construction when I was in Albania in 1984, but was closed by NATO during the Kosovo Crisis in the 1990s. Its buckled tracks had become engulfed by vegetation. The line had become unusable. We followed numerous country lanes that led towards the lake, crossing the railway tracks each time, but long before they reached the shore all of them deteriorated into unappealing farm tracks, unsuitable for cars and unattractive for pedestrians.

Entering Shkodër, we passed a roundabout. In the middle of it, there was a splendid monument consisting of five soldiers bristling with weaponry, each facing in a different direction. Created in 1969, this used to stand in Shkodër's central square near the Rozafa Hotel. According to Michael Harrison, who studies Albanian monuments, this one commemorates 'The 5 Heroes of Vig', who went to the small mountain village of Vig in August 1944 in order to:

"...talk to the peasants who were under the thumb of the feudal chief, Gjon Markagjoni, 'a tool of the fascist occupiers'" to persuade them to support the Communist partisans.

Incidentally, Markagjoni, an Anti-Communist, was described favourably by Oakley-Hill, who knew him well, and, also, warmly by Ann Bridge in her novel *Singing Waters* (published 1946, but based on her visit to Albania during the 1930s, when she accepted Markgjoni's hospitality).

After parking in Shkodër and drinking in the Pedonalje, we strolled around the old city. We wanted to reach a mock mediaeval clock tower topped with crenellations, which we had noticed while driving through the town. Finding this building took a bit of doing even though we were very close to it. The tower is attached to a two-storey stone building with shuttered windows. This house was built in the nineteenth century by an Englishman named 'Lord Paget'.

The Shkodër based photographers, the Marubi brothers, produced a picture entitled *Major George Thomas Cavendish Paget in Albanian Costume*. According to his obituary in the London *Times* dated 30th January 1939, he was born in 1853, and was in northern Albania at the outbreak of the Greco-Turkish War in 1897. Robert Elsie wrote in his *A Biographical Dictionary of Albanian History*:

"Paget settled in Shkodra where he lived sporadically in the so-called Paget Villa that was financed by his father as a headquarters for Protestant missionaries…"

His father was General Lord Alfred Henry Paget (1816-1888), who built an Anglican church in Shkodër in about 1868 as well as the villa. Protestantism did not catch on in northern Albania where most of the Christians were Roman Catholic. However, today Protestant missionaries are again active in the region.

In the 1940s, Edith Durham wrote in an article that "George Paget's house in Shkodër" was still standing. It continues to do so today long after her death. George Paget, like Edith Durham, was a member of the Albanian Committee in London, which was a forerunner of the still extant Anglo-Albanian Association that was founded around 1913. Paget's villa in Shkodër used to house an ethnographic museum until 1990. Long before that, its tower, known in Albanian as 'Kulla inglizit' (the Englishman's Tower), had clocks, the outlines of which can still be seen. Following Enver Hoxha's orders, these were removed and installed in the castle of Gjirokastër.

We ate dinner at Oborri Shkodran ('Shkodran courtyard'), a spacious restaurant with a garden. Our meal included excellent seafood soup and pasta with *fruits de mer*. We also enjoyed a speciality of the city consisting of deep-fried slices of aubergine rolled around a stuffing of ham and cheese.

Monument (at Bahçallëk near Shkodër) to the reconstruction after the 1979 earthquake. The houses behind were built just after the 'quake. The Rozafa Castle can be seen top right on the hill top.

The Ottoman bridge at Mesi

Road from Lake Shkodër to Bogë and Shala in 'High Albania'

Shirokë, Zogaj, Vau-i-dejës, Pukë, Shkodër

Wednesday, 25th May 2016 We drove to the south-western edge of Shkodër, crossing the River Buna by the newest of two bridges. A small suburb of Shkodër lies on the left bank of the Buna at the base of Mount Tarabosh, a high ridge that extends from the Buna westwards towards, and then across, the Montenegrin border. The tireless Ottoman traveller Evliya Çelebi (1611-1682) visited Shkodër, and noted that:

"Mount Tarabosh, which looms up from the other side of the lake, is a cannon's range distance. It was from there that Mehmet the Conqueror bombarded the fortress."

This would have been in 1478-79 during the Siege of Shkodër, which concluded as a Turkish victory but not without great numbers of lives being lost by the Albanians, Venetians and the Turks. Çelebi also notes that the inhabitants of Shkodër: "... all speak Albanian, which is like no other tongue." In his opinion, the Albanians were in origin:

"... one of the Arab tribes of Quryash in Mecca. That is why there are still some Arabic words still in use among them. When these Albanian tribesmen emerged from the mountains of Shkodër and Vlora, they mingled with the Italian Franks, and so, during the Caliphate of Umar, produced a language between Arabic and Frankish."

Interesting as this might seem, few if any would agree with Çelebi nowadays. The Turkish writer follows this introduction to Albanian with some 'useful phrases', including some that he regarded as "... foolish expressions, but the traveller needs to know them since he might be the object of cursing or a beating..." One of the politer examples that he noted was "ti pirishte bihund" (in modern Albanian: *Unë do të pjerdh në hundë*), which he translates as "I'll fart in your nose."

We parked next to the older bridge. This was the only one that existed when I visited Albania in 1984. However, it was not nearly as old as that which Edward Lear saw in 1848:

"... constructed of pointed arches of irregular width, and having the effect of the columns of a cathedral, suddenly resolved on crossing the stream, some with little steps, some with long..."

A new mosque was under construction close by. Near this, we saw some simple shops and a café, where dark complexioned Roma ('gypsy') people were gathered. There was a shanty town by the river next to the mosque where many of them lived.

The old bridge was still in use. It looked like a Bailey Bridge such as those developed by the Americans and British during WW2 for rapid, often temporary, bridge construction. Its 'roadway' consisted of planks, many of which were either rotting or even missing. This did not deter a steady stream of cyclists, motorcyclists, and pedestrians from using it. Several anglers were fishing from the bridge, leaning their rods against its riveted iron railings, reminding me of the anglers who line the Galata Bridge in Istanbul. The view from the bridge looking north towards Lake Shkodër was like a Chinese painting. In the distant background, we saw mountains, which appeared to merge with the puffy clouds that gathered around their summits. In the foreground, leafy trees stood in the still waters of the lake, which had become swollen during the recent heavy rains.

We followed the southern shore of Lake Shkodër towards the Montenegrin frontier, passing a lakeside resort, Shirokë. We had hoped to catch a glimpse of the summer palace that used to belong to King Zog, but we did not. Since returning to London, I have discovered that the palace still exists, but not as close to the lake as where we were looking. Our road wound picturesquely along the lake shore towards the village of Zogaj, about a kilometre from Montenegro.

Beehive at Zogaj

We drove through Zogaj until the road ended at a parking place next to a mosque by the lakeshore. There was a middle-aged Albanian couple sitting by the lake. They followed us into the grounds of the mosque. They were locals who had been to this spot often, but had never thought of trying to open the gate to the grounds surrounding the mosque. By passing through the gate, we obtained a good view of the Montenegrin shore and the rows of mountains rising behind it. We saw some small rocky islands in the lake, all of them Montenegrin. The couple spoke to us in Italian. They pointed out a ruined outhouse next to the mosque. It was full of beehives, each one surrounded by swarms of busy bees. A hedgehog that looked stunned sat on its hind legs, apparently sniffing the air, or maybe breathing its last.

While we enjoyed the view, we chatted with the couple. They were both retired. They said that they had learnt Italian by watching Italian television illicitly during the Communist era. There had been a powerful TV transmitter on the Montenegrin (then Yugoslav) side of the border, and its transmissions could be picked up in the Shkodër area. During summer months when many Italians visited Montenegro, this transmitter broadcasted Italian TV channels. By watching these, many Albanians in the area gradually learnt Italian. I was once told by an Albanian correspondent that during the Communist times the TV sets available in Albania were programmed only to receive Albanian TV stations. However, an illegally-made device could be fitted so that any programme could be watched. I asked the couple about this, but they had never heard of it. They explained that Italian TV programmes had provided Albanians a window to the world outside Hoxha's hermetically sealed country. Having watched some Italian television during the decades of the Communist regime, I wondered what the Albanians made of the world portrayed so strangely in these programmes.

We left our new acquaintances to resume gazing at the lake, and then drove into Zogaj, where we stopped at a small bar. Inside, two large television screens were placed so that they faced each other on opposite walls. One of them was showing an Albanian TV channel without sound; the other was showing a Montenegrin pop music channel with the sound turned right up.

We enjoyed cool drinks on the café's sun-drenched veranda. It faced a narrow stony staircase that climbed steeply between old houses on the hillside. I visited the toilet in the café. When Lopa wanted to use it, the barman entered first, and then emerged bearing a cage containing a small yellow bird. It had been in the 'loo' when I was there, but I had not noticed it because it was not singing in my presence. Despite the blaring Montenegrin music that resembled the Yugoslav rock music from the 1980s, or maybe because of it, the bird began chirping enthusiastically.

Below the café, a short concrete jetty extended out over the lake. There were six anglers on it, catching fish at a good rate. We asked one of them if the fish were for market, and learned that they were for consumption at their homes. One of the men had dark skin and grey curly hair typical of a black African or an Afro-Caribbean. Every now and then, he chatted in Albanian to the other fishermen. I would have loved to have spoken to him, but manners held me back. I did not want to make him feel awkward by asking him why he was there. Later, an Albanian friend speculated that he might have a descendant of African slaves that the Turks brought to Albania during the Ottoman period. There are the remnants of a small 'black' community, descendants of slaves who arrived four hundred years ago, living in Ulcinj (Montenegro). I have also read that some of the few 'black' people living near Lake Shkodër and in a few other parts of the Balkans might possibly have ancestors who arrived with the Romans. Sir Henry Holland (1788- 1873) wrote of Ioannina, which was an important administrative centre in Ottoman Albania, in his *Travels in the Ionian Isles, Albania, Thessaly, Macedonia, &c., during the years 1812 and 1813*:

"The population of Ioannina thus variously composed, and with the addition of Arabs Moors and Negroes, affords a curious spectacle in all of the streets of the city. Somewhat such an assemblage may be seen in other Turkish towns…"

And, until 1912, every town in Albania was a "Turkish town", and therefore might have had some 'negroes' living in them.

We sped cross-country to join a road that led to Pukë, which is not on most tourists' itineraries. Before leaving London, I had thought it would be interesting to visit a few places that were not obvious tourist attractions in order to see how 'ordinary', rather than 'tourist', Albania had changed since Communist times. To reach Pukë, we had to drive through Vau-i-Dejës (in Albanian 'vau' means ford). As we approached the small town, numerous police cars with blue flashing lights raced past us in the opposite direction. They were escorting limousines which, we imagined, were transporting VIPs.

When we reached Vau-i-Dejës, we joined a traffic jam. Vehicles were crawling slowly through a vast crowd of people milling on the street. Some of them were wearing traditional costumes, and many were in sombre mourning clothes. There were many priests and nuns amongst them. Eventually, we reached a point in the centre of the town where the road turned, and there we saw a newly built cathedral from which many people were emerging including quite a few nuns wearing the garb of the Order of Mother Teresa. A well-attended service had just ended. It had been a funeral service for Monsignor Luciano Agostini, the Bishop of the Diocese of Sape, a suffragan (subordinate bishop) of the Metropolitan Archdiocese of Shkodër. The service had been attended by high-level government personalities including Dr Sali Berisha, who has served Albania both as its Prime Minister and as its President. Hence, the police escort that we witnessed. Agostini (1963-2016) was born in Ferizaj (aka Uroševac) in what is now Kosovo. He had been a priest in Prizren (in Kosovo) between 1986 and 2006, and then moved to Vau-i-Dejës. A believer in inter-religious harmony, he offered great assistance to

Kosovar refugees during the Kosovo Crisis in the late 1990s. He was much loved amongst Albanians.

Having passed through the crowds, we speeded up as we pulled out of Vau-i-Dejës and away from the coastal plain. We travelled through forested hilly country. There were high mountain peaks on the horizon in whichever direction we looked. It was during this journey that we first noticed that the branches of many of the numerous conifer trees were covered with what resembled large white cotton-wool balls, rather like fluffy Christmas decorations. They consisted of complex woven bundles of fine filaments attached to a light brown solid tuber-like base. I learnt that these are the 'homes' of tent caterpillars. Julian Hoffman, a naturalist who lives close to Albania in north-west Greece, said that they are the 'Pine processionary' variety. The caterpillars hatch from eggs laid within these things in the trees. They are detrimental to the health of the trees because they make excursions from their tents to devour leaves. After about six to eight weeks, the caterpillars become moths, which then lay fresh eggs. The eggs hatch, and then after young caterpillars emerge from their pupae, they create their 'tents'.

The sky clouded over. Our road climbed up to the top of a pass, and then snaked steeply downwards into a valley. We crossed this along the narrow roadway on top of a tall slender viaduct near Gomsiqe. It traversed a river, which was flowing far below us in a deep rocky ravine. Once across the river, we began winding our way up another forested hill. We saw almost no buildings until we had crossed another pass, and descended into a gloomy little settlement called Kçirë. It consisted of a number of bleak apartment blocks from the Communist era, all in need of repair. They had patches of deteriorating plasterwork through which brickwork showed, rusting satellite-TV dishes, and many windows with broken panes. At first, we thought the place was deserted, but when I stopped to take photographs, we saw a man emerging from one of these blocks. This forlorn little place had one tiny shop, which was closed, otherwise there seemed to be little going for it.

Kcirë was amongst the places in the area that the Catholic cleric Dom Suma Ndoc (1877-1958), served as Parish Priest before he was arrested by the Communists in December 1946 whilst celebrating mass. After being released from prison in 1954, he went into hiding, celebrating mass clandestinely in Pistull, which is about eight kilometres from Vau-i-dejës. Even though Enver Hoxha forbade *all* religious activity only in 1967, he had already begun persecuting clerics long before, as, for example, Zef Pllumi described in his book *Live to Tell*.

We arrived in Pukë. Eight hundred and ninety metres above sea level, it is one of the higher towns in the country. One of the first buildings that we saw was the Shkolla 9-Vjecare (meaning '9-year school', which offers students a nine-year long programme of education). The beautiful restoration of this school, was financed, so a notice informed us, by an Austrian based organisation, which has also assisted other projects in Pukë. The school was named 'Migjeni' in honour of a great Albanian poet. For a brief period in the 1930s, Migjeni (born in Shkodër as: Millosh Gjergj Nikolla), who died aged 28, worked as a head teacher at a school in Pukë (but not the one we saw). Although he was educated in Slav language schools, including a Macedonian seminary, and raised in the southern Slav intellectual milieu, he wrote his poetry (and prose) in Albanian. Lyricism and romanticism were not for him. His poetry is dark, questioning the fundamentals of life, often remarking on its hopelessness and futility. During the Communist era, when artistic expression was rigidly controlled by ideological considerations, Migjeni's poetry was taught in schools. He continues to be highly regarded in contemporary Albanian life.

The temperature had dropped. We were cold and hungry. Someone directed us to the Univers, a Restaurant on the ground floor of one of the town's many well-maintained Communist era blocks of flats. The dining room was crowded. Most of the tables were occupied by men in uniform with machine-guns, pistols, and bullet-proof waistcoats. They were members of the FNSH, the special armed police force of Albania – the elite of the country's security forces, and they were enjoying hearty lunches. We found a table, and ordered food from one of the two busy waiters. We were served one of the best meals that we ate during our stay in Albania. We had: a wonderful mixed 'village salad' that included lettuce, tomatoes, cucumber, onions, gherkins, good feta cheese, and the nicest kaçkavalli cheese that I have ever eaten; vegetable soup; pilaff; and superb grilled veal. While we were eating, small children playing unsupervised in the street pressed their faces against the windows to watch what was going on in the restaurant. They did not look starved or unkempt, only curious. Halfway through our meal, four men in elegant civilian suits entered the restaurant, and sat down at a table next to ours before ordering raki and food. Lopa noticed that when one of them moved, his double-breasted jacket opened a little, just enough to see that he was wearing a large black gun in a shoulder holster.

After lunch, we looked at a dejected grey concrete monument bearing a red star. It was close to the school and surrounded by uninviting garden benches, which were missing most of their wooden slats. The monument recorded that on March the 2nd 1942, Pukë established its anti-fascist youth organization.

All the buildings along the town's main street dated from the Communist era or before, and were well-cared for. Many of them were painted in yellow ochre, a colour that was favoured in the Communist period. Some buildings in side streets were not so well looked after, but many of them had flower-filled gardens. The town was neat, tidy, and nicely laid out. Large trees thick with foliage lined some of the pavements to provide shade in the hot summer months. We saw a barber's shop on the main street, which had a brush and a pair of scissors painted on its external wall. Between them, there was a painting of a candle with a flame, suggesting that singeing was available. When I was a little boy in London in the late 1950s, I remember that my barber, Mr Pearce, in Golders Green used to singe the ends of hairs with lighted tapers (to seal split-ends) – a malodorous procedure.

We entered a wonderfully chaotic looking hardware shop. Its shelves were crowded with all kinds of tools and other products and a huge variety of lights hanging from the ceiling, but its shopkeeper knew exactly where everything was. We wanted to buy a reading lamp, because the two places that we had slept in so far did not provide them. We left the shop without having bought a lamp, but instead a screw-driver (with a gaudy stars and stripes handle) to replace one of many which we have 'lent' builders working in our home.

Our shopping expedition continued in a tiny stationery/gift shop, where I bought a notebook. The sales lady wanted to know where we came from. When she learnt that Lopa came from India, she pointed at a small television set hidden under her counter. We saw that she was watching a Bollywood movie with Albanian subtitles. Every afternoon on Albanian television, there is an episode of a Bollywood TV soap opera. Those 'in the know' never ring ladies between certain hours in the afternoon so as not to disturb their enjoyment of this addictive show. The inter-continental cultural traffic is not one-way: in 2013, the Albanian actress Denisa Gokovi starred in a film (*Phir Mulaquat Ho Na Ho*) directed by the Indian Bobby Sheik.

We had parked outside an internet café located in the ground floor of a Hoxha era building. Had internet have been available during the dictator's 'reign', I am certain that it would have only been available to a very select few, as it is in North Korea. As we left Pukë, we remarked that so far no one had stared at us as being strangers or bothered us in any way at all, apart from lackadaisical gypsy beggars. We returned by the mountainous road that we had arrived on. Before reaching the sad village of Kçirë, we encountered a country lady leading her four cows along the road. On many roads in rural Albania, just as in rural India that we know well, we met farmers (usually accompanied by dogs) leading their (often quite large) picturesque herds and flocks. Commonly, these animals and a small plot of land were all that sustained poor country families. Everywhere we ate, we were told that the delicious food that we were served was sourced locally, the meat and dairy products coming from the animals that we saw moving along the highways and byways, and grazing on the verdant slopes of the hills that we traversed.

When we arrived back in Vau-i-dejës, all was quiet. The morning crowds had gone. The place looked deserted. We entered a thatch-covered building, the Nacional Restaurant, which looked like a traditional African dwelling, a larger than average rondavel, and entered its circular bar. Apart from the barman and the inevitable small caged-bird, which was positioned next to a stuffed ram's head and an old-fashioned butter churn, there was a young Albanian man who spoke German. He had worked for three years in Leipzig. He was one of many Albanians who have worked, or still work, outside Albania. Their earnings are an important source of income for their families, who remain at home in Albania. Since 1990, the country has been severely depopulated as a result of Albanians seeking work abroad. Plenty of the new building construction that can been seen all over the country is financed by money earned beyond its borders.

Many buildings in Albania look unfinished because naked, often corroded, steel concrete-reinforcement rods protrude from their flat roofs. This puzzled Lopa. I told her that many years ago (before 1980) someone in Greece, where this phenomenon was commonly seen, explained to me that no tax was chargeable on unfinished buildings, and these rods were left protruding to signify that a building was not yet (or might never be) eligible for tax. An article in the *Oslo Times*, dated 4th September 2013, offered other suggestions for these unfinished buildings including the possibilities that they have either been left ready for future enlargement or:

"... that many of these buildings are built illegally without planning permission and they may have been stopped altogether."

Yet another explanation (see: http://architecturelab.net/, dated 27th June 2016) is that many buildings were built in the early 1990s before the collapse of the pyramid investment schemes, but remained unfinished because of the collapse. This is possible, but many buildings started long after 1997 have also been left looking unfinished.

We arrived back at Shkodër after having driven along a minor road past some hemi-circular reservoirs, part of a hydroelectric scheme on the River Drin between Meda and Guri-i-zi. Well-watered and mountainous, Albania is ideal for hydroelectric projects.

Paget's villa and tower in central Shkodër. Note the circular blank clock face frames.

The old bridge across the River Buna at Shkodër. Note the railings, which resemble those on Bailey bridges.

Barber shop in Pukë. The candle may indicate that hair singeing is available here.

Tirana, Elbasan

Thursday, 27th May 2016 To reach Elbasan from Shkodër by road, it was necessary to drive via Tirana. We joined the by-pass that ran around the western side of the capital. However, we had to leave it soon because it was blocked by major roadworks: a new flyover was being constructed at a point halfway around it. We followed a diversion along with much heavy traffic. It took us into the heart of the city, which we had hoped to avoid. We drove alongside the River Lana, passing the huge fortified Russian Embassy in the Bllok and the Pyramid of Enver Hoxha. There were frequent traffic signals that allowed only a few vehicles to pass on each green light. After travelling bumper-to-bumper at snail's pace, we left the city along Rruga e Elbasanit, passing the café where we had drunk coffee with our friend Shemsi. As we gained distance from the city centre, the traffic lightened, and soon we arrived at a huge roundabout, which we had to circumnavigate a couple of times as it was not clear to us which of several roads led to Elbasan by the route we had chosen.

In 1984, there was only one road to Elbasan from the capital, and that traversed the difficult, steep Krabbe Pass. Today, there is new tunnel built beneath the mountains over which the old road crosses. This new tunnel has shortened the time taken to drive between Tirana and Elbasan by about two hours. We wanted to go the old, more scenic way. Because a new motorway - the approach road to the tunnel - was under construction, all traffic had to follow the old, badly-maintained narrow road between Tirana and the tunnel.

Near the village of Mullet, we pulled into the Riz Resort. This attractive hotel complex is on the River Erzen just below the castle at Petrela, which stands high on a hill across the river. We had a pleasant luncheon in the hotel's garden close to the river. A hen with her brood of chickens fussed about near our table. Weeks later, I read that the bodies of twenty-two innocent intellectuals, murdered on the orders of Enver Hoxha in February 1951, were buried in an unmarked grave by the Erzen. The pretext for killing them was the alleged discovery of a small amount of explosive at the Embassy of the USSR in Tirana.

We continued beyond Mullet to Mushqeta, where a short new road leading to the tunnel branched off the old road. After taking a few wrong turnings and getting unhelpful advice from a group of drunk young men who were using a petrol station as a makeshift bar, we began tackling the scenic old route over the mountains to Elbasan. We met hardly any other traffic.

Soon after crossing the boundary between the Counties of Tirana and Elbasan, we stopped to enjoy the view from the small settlement of Gracen. We parked next to a ramshackle eatery that was emitting the delicious smells of grilling meat. Several donkeys tethered in a field above the road watched us whilst we admired the panorama from the high ridge where we were standing. We marvelled at the profusion, a colourful tapestry, of wild flowers around us. Then, we drove past an elaborately carved memorial to someone killed on the road in 1997. Similar tragic reminders of the hazards of driving are to be found all over Albania. They are rapidly outnumbering the so-called '*lapidari*', stone or concrete monuments erected during the Communist era to honour those who had been killed during WW2.

The old road ran along the crest of a high mountain ridge until it was almost directly above Elbasan. Then, it descended towards the plain of Elbasan along a well-engineered series of hairpin bends. When Edward Lear approached Elbasan in September 1848 (from the east, rather than the west as we were doing), he wrote:

"… and after another hour's ride through widening uncultivated valleys, and Elbasan is in sight, lying among groves of olives on a beautiful plain, through which the Skumbi, an unobstructed broad torrent, flows to the Adriatic."

The river still flows today, but the landscape has changed dramatically. From each of the hairpin bends on our descent, we had spectacular views over the plain described by Lear. Gone are the olive groves. In their place, we beheld an immense industrial wasteland. It had been Albania's metallurgical complex (built with Chinese assistance). It is now a vast expanse of ruined buildings with missing windows that made me think of eye-sockets in skulls. The area, which has numerous brick and concrete chimney stacks, was once the pride of Albanian industry. Its decline, following the ending of Chinese assistance, was described in Ismail Kadare's fascinating novel *The Concert*. It is not yet totally dead. Some industrial activity including a little processing of chromium is still occurring, but what remains is a pale shadow its former glory.

We drove into the city of Elbasan, a place that I only visited for only about an hour or two in 1984, when all that I saw was the outside of the city's then disused cathedral. We took a wrong turn, and ended up at a park with a rusting gate that bore the word 'Park Dëshmorëteve' (Martyr's Park). Beyond it, I glimpsed a Communist-style war memorial. We made a U-turn, and arrived at the city's high castle walls, which were built by the Ottomans using masonry from Roman and other earlier buildings. With help from passers-by we found our way into the well-hidden car park of the Real Scampis Hotel, whose name has nothing to do with seafood. Its restaurant had a huge garden enclosed by the castle walls. The pleasant garden, which contained some archaeological remains, had tables and chairs on number of terraces overlooking it.

As we were too early to meet our friends, we explored the narrow streets of old Elbasan, and visited the Xhamia-i-mbretit, the King's Mosque (aka Xhamia Sulltan Bajazit). Built by 1492 and restored by the Turks after the end of Communism, it is one of the oldest mosques in the Balkans. On our way back to the Scampis I noticed that the cobbled street along which we were walking, lined with lovely old houses, was named 'Rruga Egnatia'. We were on a short section of the Via Egnatia, the road built by ancient Romans to connect Durrës, to Constantinople (Istanbul) via Thessaloniki. The Romans knew Elbasan as 'Scampis'.

When Edward Lear arrived in Elbasan in late September 1848, he encountered problems when trying to make sketches. He wrote:

"No sooner had I settled to draw ... than forth came the populace of Elbasan ... there were soon from eighty to a hundred spectators collected, with earnest curiosity in every look; and when I had sketched one of the principal buildings as they could recognise a universal shout of 'Shaitan' [i.e. devil] burst from the crowd ... one of those tiresome Dervishes – in whom, with their green turbans, Elbasan is rich – soon came up, and yelled, Shaitan scroo! – Shaitan!' [i.e. The Devil draws! – the Devil!] in my ears with all his force; seizing my book also..."

Our friends Sar and Nick met us, as planned, in the car park of the hotel with their two sons: Daniel and Jonathan. We were going to follow their car on our journey to their home outside Elbasan. Before setting off, I asked Nick whether he thought that our Tata car would suitable for the rustic roads that we would have to drive along. He took a quick glance at it, and then said that he thought it was. However, as we proceeded I began to have my doubts. Daniel got into our car with us, so that if we became separated from Nick and Sar's vehicle he could tell us the way. He was a great travelling companion, explaining many interesting things as we drove.

We followed Nick past the ruined metallurgical complex along a good road to its junction with another leading towards Cerrik. Soon after crossing a river, we passed cultivated fields along a poorly surfaced road. We had to stop for a few minutes to allow first an enormous flock of goats, and then another of sheep, to pass us. Bumpy as this road was, it was nothing compared to what was to come. We followed Nick along a steadily rising, deeply rutted mountain dirt track that was strewn with small boulders and fragments of rocks with jagged edges. I was convinced that we would puncture a tire, or, worse, damage the underside of our car. Daniel kept making reassuring comments, and some less reassuring ones, such as informing us on a regular basis there was another hour's driving ahead. He pointed at two slender antennae far above us on the summit of a high mountain, and then told us that his home was close to them. Meanwhile, I tried to steer our vehicle to avoid particularly nasty looking pot-holes and boulders, and, at one point, an exposed large-diameter metal pipe that had created a steep step in the road.

One track led to another, each one worse than the previous. Yet, we appeared to be making hardly any progress. The two antennae always seemed a long way off. Nick stopped outside a farmhouse to chat (in Albanian) to its owner. Daniel informed us that this farmer was one of their neighbours. This raised my flagging spirits temporarily until I remembered that neighbours in the countryside do not always live close to each other.

Eventually, we arrived at our hosts' house, perched high above sea-level on the top of a hill (almost a mountain) amidst a lovely garden. Sar and Nick and their sons and Val, an American lady living with the family, were perfect hosts. Sar and Nick have been living in Albania and doing valuable social work there almost since the fall of the Communist regime. Sar served us delicious roasted goat with potatoes and salad, followed by locally grown strawberries and cherries. During the meal, we learnt about a ring that had been found by an Albanian man in about 1960 near the spot where a RAF Halifax bomber had crashed into a 6000-foot-high mountain during WW2. Afraid to report his discovery during the Hoxha era, Jaho Cala kept the wedding ring hidden for decades. After 1990, he asked his son Xhemil, who had become a policeman, to discover who had owned the ring because he wanted to return it. After much research, it was revealed that the ring had belonged to a British airman, Sergeant Thompson. He was killed in the crash in 1944 soon after his marriage. In 2015, long after his widow had died, the ring was presented to the airman's elderly sister.

Over dinner, we talked about the district around us. Many houses in the area where Sar and Nick lived were having to be extensively rebuilt. They had been constructed in the Communist period using substandard breeze blocks, which were now beginning to dissolve into dust. On our way up the mountain, we had noticed the local school had many broken windows. One of the boys explained that this was not caused by neglect, but because children in one class delighted in breaking the windows of the other children's classrooms. We learnt that local people suffered from a lack of economic opportunities. Once, things began to look up when many of villagers worked for several months on a local hydro-electric project. Tragically, when the work was done, the workers were never paid for their labour. Life in Albania is still not at all easy.

After dinner, Daniel and his brother played music for us on their saxophone and keyboards. We were very touched when the family joined together to sing for us. Although we had only met Sar once before, and briefly at that, we felt that by meeting her family we had made some great new friends.

Before falling asleep, I perused one of our hosts' books. Written by Edwin Jacques and David Young and published by the Albanian Evangelical Mission, *Battle for Albania* was about religion in Albania. I read that when he 'abolished' religion, Enver Hoxha claimed that he was against the Muslims because they had collaborated with the Turks; the Orthodox because they had worked with the Greeks; and the Catholics because they had allied with the Italians. This nonsense was backed up by his notion that by abandoning religion, the Albanian people would be more easily united. Long before Hoxha dreamt this up and then turned it into a national nightmare, Albanians of all religions had been united: they considered themselves, and still do, primarily Albanians, and secondarily followers of a one or other religion.

Hoxha abolished religion in late 1966, and then began persecuting the clergy in early 1967. This was soon after Mao Tse Tung had launched China's Cultural Revolution. His ally Enver Hoxha decided not only to emulate it in Albania, but also to 'improve' on it by extinguishing all religious activity in his country. Many clerics were killed cold-bloodedly or incarcerated. Even possession of a holy book or utterance of religious sentiments could result in imprisonment in harsh labour camps. Many religious buildings and artefacts were destroyed. Fortunately, Hoxha's experiment in creating the world's first atheist state failed to destroy the soul of the Albanian people.

Stopping to allow sheep to pass. Near Elbasan

On the Via Egnatia in central Elbasan. Note the graffiti.

Elbasan, Lin, and Pogradec

Friday, 28th May 2016 After breakfast, ably prepared and elegantly served by Daniel and John, they took us on a tour of their far from horizontal garden. We admired fruit trees, geese, ducks, beehives, and their very own concrete bunker left over from the Hoxha-era. They had made it comfortable, and used it to shelter from summer heat. Incidentally, many of the bunkers lining Albania's beaches have been converted into unusual beach huts, where Albanians can get protection from the sun rather than from hostile armies. The views from the garden were superb. In one direction, there were ranges of wooded hills beyond which the city of Elbasan could be seen dissolving in the heat haze. In another, the sinuous River Shkumbin snaked across the plain of Elbasan. The river has a linguistic significance. South of it, most Albanians speak the Tosk dialect of their language, whereas north of it (and, also, in Kosovo) the Gheg dialect predominates. Enver Hoxha, a Tosk speaker, ensured that the official written language of modern Albania became Tosk. It remains thus today.

With much trepidation, we entered our Tata, and then began the hair-raising descent from our friends' home. Descending was no easier than ascending. Near the school with its broken windows, I remembered the exposed drainpipe and manoeuvred gingerly around it. Had I forgotten it, we might have become grounded. Years before, I grounded a car in the city of Orange in France. Even though there was a garage a few metres away, it took a long time to rescue the car, and then to repair its ruptured fuel line. Had this happened on this remote track, our subsequent journey might have been different to what we had planned. I breathed a long sigh of relief when, much more than one hour after leaving our friends, we were at last driving on a decent tarmac road. The car was still intact. The experience was not wasted; driving on those mountains was a baptism of fire - it prepared us for coping with some of the challenging roads that we would encounter later.

From Elbasan, we joined the main road that leads towards Qafe e Thane (*qafe* means pass). At the summit of this pass, the road splits: one branch going south towards Pogradec and Korçë, and the other going vaguely north-east towards Macedonia. For most of the way, the road followed the River Shkumbin up its picturesque valley. A disused railway track that connected Elbasan and Pogradec followed much the same course as the road. Once, it carried chromium ore from Pogradec to the metallurgical complex at Elbasan, but no longer. Hugging the mountain slopes, it traversed numerous bridges and passed through many tunnels.

We had lunch at Hotel Resort Ballkan near Elbasan at Labinot Fushë. During WW2, a couple of conferences were held in Labinot to establish the supremacy of the Communist-led partisans over the others – the Zogists (pro King Zog) and the Nationalists (they were opposed to Zog and the Communists). From our table in the hotel's garden, we saw the turquoise blue water of the River Shkumbin rushing past. This made more of an impression on me than the meal we ate. After lunch, we passed the town of Librazhd and then, after following the river for a few more kilometres, our road left the valley and began ascending a pass. We stopped just east of Prrenjas, a small town in a plain surrounded by high peaks, and entered a small simple café made of wood, like a log cabin. It was mid-afternoon. A couple of workmen were sitting at a nearby table eating *paçe* soup, which they washed down with carbonated drinks. Next door to the café there was a public water spring.

There was a gravelly parking area outside the café, where cars, vans, and trucks were being washed by young men wielding long hoses. Across the road, there were other men waving hoses gushing water. They were trying to attract motorists to have their vehicles washed. Car washing, or '*lavazh*' as it is called in Albanian, is a thriving business. We saw almost as many car-wash places in Albania as cafés. Given the dusty nature of the Albanian roads in good weather and their muddiness in bad, *lavazh* is in great demand. Even in faraway London, there are car-washing businesses run by Albanians. The great thing about car-washing is that negligible outlay and minimal skill is required to set up a basic *lavazh*.

More surprising than the car-washes was the extraordinary variety of filling-stations in Albania. Many of them were sole traders, not branches of large companies. We saw much competition between neighbouring filling-stations. Even when they were close to each other, they charged different amounts for a litre of fuel. At one place near Korçë, we saw a cluster of four filling-stations, all selling fuel at widely differing prices.

While there were outlets belonging to big companies such as Gega, Alpetrol, Kastrati, and the highly-priced Italfuel, most filling-stations were unattached to larger companies. We wondered whether individuals opened their own stations, hoping that eventually they would be bought out by one of the larger companies. One Albanian suggested to us that they served a dual purpose, fuelling vehicles and at the same time doing something less legitimate. Few of the filling stations, even those that advertised they did, accepted credit cards. As with other transactions we made in Albania, cash is king.

Beyond Prrenjas, the road climbed up high mountainside. At certain spots, we had good views of large articulated trucks crawling slowly along the zig-zagging road. They travelled through Qafe e Thane on journeys between central or northern Albania and either Macedonia or southern Albania. Despite its mountainous nature, this road is the best of only four main roads that connect the northern and southern halves of Albania. One of these, the coastal road, used to be a perilous track, and has only recently been improved. The others, which pass through either Berat or Tepelenë, are not as well engineered as the one we were on.

From near Qafe e Thane, we headed towards Pogradec, and soon saw the blue waters of Lake Ohri ('Ohrid' in Macedonian) far below us. The mountains across the lake in Macedonia and the clouds above them were reflected in the still, mirror-like lake. This body of water, which is shared by Albania and Macedonia, is one of the loveliest places that I have seen in Europe. During the 1970s and 1980s, I visited its Yugoslav shores and stayed in the historic city of Ohrid. I remember the line of white buoys that used to demarcate the watery border between Yugoslavia and Albania. Now, these have disappeared, and so has Yugoslavia. In 1984, I was taken along the road from Elbasan to Pogradec, where we had lunch at a lakeside hotel. At that time, I thought that Pogradec was drab compared to places like Ohrid and Struga on the Yugoslav shore. We discovered that this was no longer true.

We descended to the narrow band of flattish land by the lake, and turned off the main road to visit the charming, small fishing village of Lin. It nestles on a finger-like rocky promontory sticking out into the lake. We drove through the village along its narrow main street until it ended abruptly. While we parked our Tata, we were watched by two elderly ladies dressed in dark clothes. They were sitting beside the brick outer walls of their houses, enjoying the shade of overhead vines.

We had stopped next to a car with UK registration plates, which was being unloaded by a young man. He was a Kosovar, who works in London. His wife's family, whom he was visiting, live in Lin. He was brought up in a village close to the frontier between Kosovo and Serbia. For many years, he had to study in in secret, in illegal Kosovan schools hidden in people's houses because the Yugoslav authorities did not want Kosovar Albanians to receive education in Albanian. This surprised me because I had believed that when Kosovo was part of Yugoslavia, not only was Albanian a recognised language but the region had officially sanctioned universities. It was like that until the late 1980s, by which time Milosevic had become the 'helmsman' of the Yugoslav people. According to Fred Abrahams, author of *Modern Albania*, Milosevic agreed (with the USA and others) in September 1996 to lift his six-year closure of Albanian schools in Kosovo, but he broke his promise. In any case, our new acquaintance left Kosovo just before the bloody conflict between the Serbs and the Albanian Kosovars began in the late 1990s. He told us that his family home was ransacked by Serbian troops. When his family returned to it after living as refugees in Macedonia, they discovered that it had been booby-trapped with explosives, which would have been detonated when any light switch was turned on. Luckily for them, the electricity supply had failed.

Lin was a sleepy place on that warm afternoon. We strolled along its main street. On one side of the road, the houses were backed by a steep cliff, and on the other side by the lake. Small alleyways shaded by overhead vines led between houses to the water's edge. Where they ended, there was often a rowing boat moored on the smooth water covered with floating leaves. Lin has a small mosque and a pretty little church. Wherever we looked, we saw leafy vines. They were growing on walls, on wires crossing the street and, also on poles that projected upwards from the roofs of buildings. The place was full of flowering plants and bushes with berries. There were few people on the street. Groups of women and girls chatted outside their houses under the trellises of the vines.

From Lin, we followed the lakeshore towards Pogradec in search of the Hotel Victoria, where we had booked. We knew that it should be by the lake a little north of Pogradec, but failed to spot it. At intervals along the road, young men flapped dead fish at us, trying to attract us to stop and buy the fish that swam in tanks of murky water placed by their feet.

When we reached the outskirts of Pogradec, we knew that we had gone too far, so we retraced our steps. We passed the extensive ruins of an industrial complex on a hillside overlooking the lake. On the wall of one abandoned building I noticed large fading upper-case letters that spelled out "GANIZIM". These were part of a partially erased Communist slogan that would have included the word "ORGANIZIM", meaning 'organize'. These letters encapsulated something about Albania: its Communist era has ended, but has not been completely erased. The building was part of a chromium mining set-up, the *raison d' être* for the now disused railway that we had followed all the way from Elbasan to Pogradec.

Near this derelict establishment, I spotted an almost hidden sign pointing the way to our hotel. We followed a black dirt track that ran between abandoned industrial buildings and some sad dwellings. Our hearts sank. After passing some scruffy children playing with a ball, we reached another sign pointing towards the lake. Then, we arrived at the hotel, which was surrounded trees and bushes. Apart from its dreary approach road, the isolated Hotel Victoria was lovely. Our comfortable room had a balcony with a wonderful view of Lake Ohri. We could see the entire Macedonian lakeshore and much of the Albanian. Below us, a garden led to the water's edge where a pair of swans were passing the time of day. Out in the lake, beds of reeds swayed gently in the early evening breeze. Beyond them, several men were rowing boats, and far across the lake we saw houses in the Macedonian village of Trpejca. A camper van owned by a German couple with a baby and an infant was parked in the garden. They were spending a month in Albania.

We had a 'sundowner' by the lake, and then ate dinner in the hotel's dining room. Valent, the hotel's owner, told us that until recently the Albanian shore of Lake Ohri had been wrecked by excessive building and unauthorised structures. Shortly before our visit to Albania, the government under the leadership of Edi Rama had demolished at least thirty unsightly constructions on the lake shore. The reason was aesthetics. When their constructions were bull-dozed or blown-up, those who had been granted permission to build were compensated financially, but those who had built illegally received nothing. Even Valent, who had been given permission to build and had somehow escaped having his building removed (perhaps because it was not considered unsightly), had not got away wholly unscathed. The reception area of his hotel had extended beyond the limits of what had been permitted on the approved building plan. When Valent was told that it must be demolished, he did it himself because he believed the government's contractors would have been less careful than him. That is why the hotel's main entrance and reception area was an untidy veranda open to the elements, with sealed-off ends of electrical cables sprouting from the floor.

Ladies sitting beneath vines at Lin (Lake Ohri)

Part of abandoned mining complex near Pogradec. Notice the partially obliterated political slogan.

City of Pogradec reflected on the waters of Lake Ohri.

Pogradec and Drilon

Saturday, 29th May 2016 At breakfast, Valent told us that the mines at Pogradec used to employ many people including his father. The latter used to cycle to work on his Chinese-made bicycle, which was a highly-prized possession in Hoxha's time. After the end of Communism, the mine-workers' families were given houses and small plots of land. In many cases, this is all that keeps some of them from starving.

We discussed the watery border on the lake. Crossing the lake to escape from Communist Albania was almost impossible. Some attempted to swim, others tried by boat. If anyone approached the border, fast speed-boats would be sent out to catch them. Valent told us that two powerful spotlights combed the lake at night: one was at Lin, and the other at Tushemisht at the southern end of the lake. He remembered seeing these in action. He told of a relative of his wife, who built a boat in secret, and managed take his family across to Yugoslavia. From there, they migrated to Australia. Even if someone managed to reach Yugoslavia, freedom was not guaranteed. The Yugoslavs needed to root out Albanian spies from genuine refugees. Valent told us that those who reached Yugoslavia were imprisoned, and questioned. To encourage the escapees to reveal whether they were spies, they were locked in a room filled with snakes. Because the terrified prisoners were unaware that the snakes were harmless, this helped the Yugoslavs to discover who was who.

We drove into Pogradec. On our way, we passed a large concrete blockhouse on the lake shore. It was quite unlike any others that we saw in Albania. I will describe it later. We parked next to a fruit-seller in a wide street that ran downhill to the lakeshore. His stall was overlooked by an old (late 19th or early 20th century) building that would have looked at home in Greek towns. The centre of Pogradec contained a pleasant mix of old buildings and newer ones, many erected during the Communist period. We walked down the street towards the lake. At its end, I saw a block of flats, which I remembered having photographed when I visited Pogradec in 1984. Then, it was plastered with political slogans; now, it is covered with commercial advertisements (see below).

Pogradec: then and now

We walked along the town's lakeside promenade, which runs next to a shady park containing a few memorials to fallen heroes and some whimsical sculptures from the Communist period. It was Saturday morning, sunny, and warm. The promenade was lively. Groups of elderly men sat around talking, pondering chess moves, playing dominoes, and one group was discussing something drawn on a large piece of paper. Parents and grandparents were out with children. Some of the youngsters were on small bicycles and tricycles. Groups of young boys were playing table-football on outdoor tables. Kiosks selling ice-creams and soft drinks were doing brisk business. One of them was cylindrical, and decorated to look like an over-sized Coca-Cola can. We stopped at a café with outdoor tables, and watched Pogradec at play. Lining the street that ran alongside the landward edge of the park, there were diverse buildings: old and new, large and small, commercial and residential. The park and promenade were supplied with small trios of rubbish bins (for the separate disposal of paper, metal, and plastic). Labels on them informed one that they had been provided by the Australian Government. About halfway along the litter-free promenade, an old building stood alone in the park. This was owned by a wealthy family and built during the reign (1928-1939) of King Zog. Further along, there was a mechanised funfair swing full of excited youngsters. This contraption bore the word "VILLIAMS" in large red illuminated Cyrillic letters.

At its southern extreme, the promenade ended abruptly at a large lakeside resort hotel called "1 Maj" (1st of May). Near to this but set back from the lake on the road that runs along the park, there was another hotel called "EuroKorçë". It looked older than the 1 Maj, and its architecture was typical of buildings that were built in the Hoxha era. I might have eaten lunch there in 1984.

Just south of the 1 Maj, we saw a large fenced-off compound that ran along the lakeshore. It contained several well-maintained ochre-painted villas, which are now occupied by the military. Inland from the fenced off area, there were fields containing derelict barrack-like buildings covered with graffiti.

Walking back to our car through the town's hot streets, we passed The Piro Xexi puppet theatre, a long low building built during the Communist period. Close by, we saw the Shkolla Koli Gusho, housed in an elegant three-storey school building. I have not discovered who Koli Gusho was, but Pogradec was the birthplace of a noted Albanian poet Lazar Gusho (1899-1987), who used the pseudonym Lasgush Poradeci. After buying some fruit, we drove south along the lakeshore towards Drilon, the penultimate Albanian village before the Macedonian border. We passed several hemispherical concrete bunkers in various states of disrepair, each one decorated with graffiti.

Soon, we spotted the signpost for Vila Art, and drove into its crowded car park. Set in lovely parkland, watered by an inlet from the lake, Vila Art is a restaurant-cum-resort housed in what had once been Enver Hoxha's lakeside summer retreat. We sat outside on a terrace under overhead trellises of complexly intertwined vines. It overlooked a pond containing swans with their grey cygnets. Near us, there was a group of lively but well-behaved teenagers, who only ordered soft drinks. We ate pork chops served in a delicious creamy wine sauce, and watched a large, well-dressed family group at a big table enjoying a birthday banquet. Whenever one of their dishes arrived, one of the smartly suited men stood up and served the rest of the party. As in so many places in Albania, there were cages containing small birds everywhere.

After lunch, we entered the building that used to be Enver Hoxha's summer 'palace'. This timber and brick construction was beautifully designed, much more attractive than Hoxha's home in Tirana's Bllok. Although the exterior of the building is what might be described as mid-twentieth century Scandinavian, the interior is cosier, more like a country club, but not old-fashioned. I was told that the ground floor, which has a bar, a lounge, and an indoor restaurant, has kept much of its original appearance.

The extensive grounds of Vila Art included a big outdoor restaurant section with tables set amongst the trees that grow alongside the water-filled inlet of the lake and the small canals branching off it. This watery network is used as a huge boating area on which groups of visitors are rowed in bulky wooden boats that looked like old-fashioned life-boats with hardly any streamlining. The waterside restaurant was well-patronised. Customers and waiters, laden with trays, dodged each other as they moved between the tables. Cages with lively small birds chirruping and hopping from perch to perch hung from many of the trees. At the edge of the park near to the car park, I saw a long single-storey building in a poor state of repair. It bore a sign saying "DISCO BAR". Possibly in Enver Hoxha's time, this housed servants or security guards.

We had a wonderful afternoon at the charming Vila Art as did everyone else we saw there. Although precious few Albanians would have had access to this place during Hoxha's lifetime, it now is open to all and sundry. General access to Vila Art helps in a minute way to compensate people for the decades of suffering they had to endure.

Near the village of Memelisht (north of Pogradec), we examined the huge bunker on the lakeshore. It was like an elongated egg in plan. Part of it protruded into the lake, and the rest caused the road to curl around it. Its entrance faced inland. Two gun slits faced north - one slightly towards the west and the other slightly towards the east. A third faced south towards Pogradec. I peered inside, and saw a central passage with doorways leading to three side rooms. The corridor was clean and painted white. A few discarded bottles lay on its floor. This 'bunker', which was so different from other bunkers that we saw in Albania, puzzled me. Valent at the hotel believed that it had been built by the Italians to control the road between Elbasan (and the north of Albania) and the south of the country, as well as Greece. This seemed reasonable. Someone in London told me that she had seen one other pre-Communist era Italian bunker beyond Tushemisht, close to the Macedonian border. I have seen a picture of this object, which has a spherical rather than ovoid shape, but it is not a Hoxha period design. It is not in Albania, but at Ljubanista (Љубаништа), just inside Macedonia, slightly west of Sveti Naum.

Back at the Hotel Victoria, we enjoyed a lazy afternoon by the still waters of Ohri. We watched swans; fishermen out in small rowing boats; examined wild flowers; and then enjoyed the ever-changing colours of the mountains across the water in Macedonia as the sun began to set. After dark, the reflections of the lights in Pogradec made colourful, rippled streaks on the surface of the lake.

Chess players on the lakeshore promenade in Pogradec

Soft drinks kiosk on the lakeshore promenade at Pogradec

Vila Art at Drilon: Enver Hoxha's former summer retreat

Tushemisht, Prespa, Bilisht, Voskopojë

Sunday, 30th May 2016 We breakfasted in Pogradec on slices of freshly-baked cheese and spinach-filled *byrek* (pastries made with layers of filo pastry interleaved with various savoury fillings: *börek* in Turkish). We ate this in a tiny shop that specialised in making it. After coffee in a minute café where a couple of men were enjoying early morning glasses of raki, we drove past the Vila Art, to Tushemisht. Nowadays, this is the last village in Albania before the Macedonian border, but it was not always. The Monastery of Sveti Naum ('Shën Naum' in Albanian) now in Macedonia is within 'spitting distance' of the border. Between 1912 and 1925, the monastery and the district around it were part of Albania. On the 28th of June 1925 because of border problems with his neighbour, King Zog 'gifted' (or possibly sold) the monastery and the land around it, which was not his to give away, to the Kingdom of Yugoslavia.

With its mixture of buildings old and new, Tushemisht was picturesque. It was full of tourists, mainly Albanian. Villagers had set up small tables outside their houses to sell home-made produce such as jams, bottled fruits, pickles, and honey. Close to the village's central square, which has several bars and cafés, we saw one of the place's main attractions: the statue of the Albanian film character 'Ollga'. With a handbag draped over her left forearm, and looking like a woman drawn by Fernando Botero or Beryl Cook, her cast-metal statue stands on a pedestal next to a water-filled pool. Visitors posed for photographs beside her. 'Teto Ollga' (Auntie Olga), as she was lovingly known by Albanian filmgoers, was portrayed by Violeta Manushi (1926-2007), a popular comedy actress who starred in many films from 1958 onwards. Her statue was like a shrine. It was in the village where at least one of her films was made. A plaque (dated 2015) stated both in Albanian and English that Manushi cherished Tushemisht, and encouraged the preservation of it and its surroundings

Some steps near the statue led up to a recently restored Orthodox church, Shën Pantelion. In front of its main entrance, we looked at two monuments. One of them praised the WW2 martyr Todi K Lushka who died in 1944. The other one bore the date 25th of May 1926, a year after territory had been given to Yugoslavia. It commemorated Dhimiter Misha, a priest who defended the Albanian language from the Cyrillic used by the 'chauvinist' (the word on the monument) Serbs at the time when the Yugoslavs were trying to disrupt the territorial integrity of Albania. The church was locked up, but its elevated position afforded good views over the village.

A stream ran through the village to some marshy, reed-filled backwaters on the edge of the settlement. Near this, one of the older houses bore a plaque stating it had once been an 'illegal' (clandestine) base of the Albanian National Liberation Front, the Communist resistance during WW2. A monument close by commemorated a struggle in April 1944 against the "Bulgarian Fascists". The village was in a much-disputed corner of the Balkans.

We drove through Pogradec, and then towards Korçë, but did not enter the city. Instead, we followed a road that runs east via Bilisht to the Albanian-Greek border. Near Zemblak, we joined a byway that headed towards the Albanian shore of Large Lake Prespa. The borders of Albania, Macedonia, and Greece, meet in the middle of this lake. It is separated from Little Lake Prespa to its south by a narrow causeway, which lies in Greek territory. When I visited this causeway in the 1970s, the Greek police recorded the names of all those who entered this part of the country so close to its then hostile neighbour, Albania.

A winding road lifted us high above the intensely cultivated plain of Korçë, a complex patchwork of elongated rectangular fields that from above resembled mediaeval strip farming on a grand scale. Dirk Bezemer wrote in *On Eagle's Wings: The Albanian Economy in Transition* that there was a return to strip farming after Communism ended. We traversed a mountain pass, and entered the Prespa National Park. The road then wound along the sides of hills mostly following a contour line. We enjoyed constantly changing views of (Large) Lake Prespa. The road led northwards to the Macedonian frontier, but we did not go that far. Direction signs in this region were trilingual. Each place name was in Albanian, Macedonian (in Cyrillic script) and a third language, which was the Latin transliteration of the Cyrillic.

We entered a small village, Goricë e Vogel (Долна Горица). Its main street was a rough unmade track. Its street name signs were bilingual as was a sign on the village's community centre building. The village contained fewer old than new buildings. There was nobody about. A couple of tethered donkeys stood close by the walls of buildings, trying to make the most of the narrow band of shade they provided. Hens, cocks, and chicklets ran about in the noonday sunshine. The calm waters of the lake shimmered in the distance beyond some fields and reed beds. There was nowhere to eat in the village, so we headed back to the larger lakeside village of Pustec (Пустец). Between 1973 and 2013, it used to be known by an Albanian name 'Liqenas'.

Some villagers directed us to a lakeside restaurant called Kristal. Overlooking the lake and with a good view of Pustec across the water, this place had been recently opened. Its owner and cook were Macedonian speaking Albanians. The former spoke good English, but the latter only spoke Macedonian (her mother tongue) and Albanian. The Albanian territory around Large Lake Prespa has been long inhabited by ethnic Macedonians with Albanian citizenship. According to the owner of the restaurant, this ethnic minority was treated badly during the Communist period.

We ate a tasty meal, which included good grilled pork chops, 'shopska' salad (a southern Slav version of 'Greek salad'), and we were offered a tasting of *salce kos* ('yoghurt sauce'; *kos* is Albanian for yoghurt). This was strained yogurt flavoured with fresh cucumber, garlic, and spicy red capsicum. I ate a traditional Albanian sweet called 'Tulumba', which is identical to a Turkish sweet with the same name. When we were 'offered' the *salce kos*, we believed that we were being given it to try rather as Juri had done when he offered us a plate of fried liver at his restaurant near Lezhë. So, we were a little surprised to find what we had not actually ordered appearing on our not very large bill. Most of the time that we were eating, a noisy group of young men on a nearby table were talking in what sounded like coarse Macedonian. They drove off in a car with Macedonian registration plates.

The owner of the restaurant told us his ambitious plans for the place. He was hoping to build what he called 'Palaeolithic huts' standing on stilts over the lake's water (with fishes underneath them) to hire out to guests. We wished him luck with this curious venture.

After lunch, I strolled along the lakeshore to get a better view of the island of Maligrad where the ruins of the Church of Shën Mërisë stand. This can be reached by boat, but when we were there the boat was out of service. As I was staring across the sunlit waters, I spotted two white birds swimming far from the shore. They were pelicans. The Prespa Lakes are an important breeding ground for the Dalmatian Pelican (*Pelecanus crispus*), which, despite their name, are not confined to Europe. Nearer the shore, I saw some black waterfowl, standing on dead branches sticking out of the water. They looked like cormorants. Later, I learnt from Julian Hoffman, who lives in Greece by Little Lake Prespa, that Prespa is home to cormorants. He told me that they often stand on perches above the water to dry out their wings. The lake in Lalbagh Gardens in the heart of Bangalore in India is also home to these birds. I have seen huge flocks of them perched on the branches of dead trees near the water. Now, I know what they are doing there.

In the centre of Pustec, we admired its large, well-maintained, traditionally designed Orthodox church. According to Pettifer in his 2001 guidebook, this church was empty in 2001, but was then beginning to be used for services even though it was in need of much restoration. He also wrote that many of the village's inhabitants are Albanian Slavs, who speak a dialect of Bulgarian. According to André Mazon writing in his *Documents contes et Chansons slaves de l'Albanie du sud*, dated 1936, the inhabitants of Pustec and the other villages by the lake used to visit the market in Korçë on Saturdays to sell fish caught in the lake and also charcoal.

Just outside Pustec, we passed some disused hemispherical concrete bunkers and a Communist WW2 memorial in a bad state of repair. The lower part of it was daubed with paint, mostly red. The highest point of it bore a double-headed eagle surmounted by a five-pointed socialist star.

Bilisht is close to the Greek border. Years ago, I bought an Italian (Touring Club Italia series) guidebook to Greece. It was published especially for the Italian troops, who were invading Greece from Italian-occupied Albania in 1941. The soldier who had owned the guidebook had marked his journey through Albania in red pencil on the book's folding map. He passed through Bilisht. So, as we were close by, we went there. On the road between Korçë and Bilisht, we passed a large hemispherical concrete bunker, of which only half remained. Its shell appeared to have been made with segments of concrete so that from the outside it looked like a quarter of a gigantic grey Terry's Chocolate Orange, resting on a circular concrete base. The smaller bunkers built in this shape were made differently. In *Between Glory and Fall* by Ilir Parangoni, there is a photograph of one of the metal moulds used to create the bowl-like cap of these reinforced concrete structures. Parangoni wrote that between 400,000 and 600,000 of these bunkers were constructed during Hoxha's 'reign'. Given that the area of Albania is 27,748 square kilometres, and using the lower figure, the density of bunkers was at least 14.4 bunkers per square kilometre. And, as they were not randomly placed, it means that in certain places there were concentrated clusters of these concrete 'pimples'. Today, many bunkers have been at least partially demolished because not only do they get in the way, but also there is a premium on the steel reinforcement metal that can be salvaged from them.

The hemispherical bunkers were designed to resist very heavy artillery. When they were being tested, some say that live animals were put inside them while the bunkers were being blasted close-range by tanks. Someone suggested that Enver Hoxha had put the bunkers' designer inside a prototype and then fired heavy explosive shells at it. The designer emerged unscathed from his invention. This might be apocryphal as is the now largely discredited belief that the builders of Roman bridges were compelled to sleep under their unfinished constructions.

We parked beside one of the town's cafés, where men were hanging about, appearing to do nothing apart from waiting for something to happen. Nobody took any interest in us. Next to the café where we parked, there was a Hoxha-era hemispherical bunker, probably placed in the centre of Bilisht to hinder invasion by Greek forces. Seeing this in the heart of the town reminded me of my visit to Shkodër in 1984. There was a similar bunker just outside the main entrance to our hotel, almost blocking it. This has been removed.

The centre of Bilisht was pleasant. Many buildings dated back to the Communist period. Some were plastered and painted, others displayed crudely finished brickwork. The upper floors of the buildings were residential. Many of the balconies of the flats were partially occupied by neatly stacked firewood. All over Albania we saw firewood being stored outdoors on balconies, suggesting that storage space in apartment blocks was at a premium. Shops and cafés occupied the raised ground floors of these apartment blocks. We saw a travel agent that advertised trips to Greece, where many Albanians work. The destinations on offer were mainly in north and central Greece, but also as far south as Athens. I noticed that the Albanian name for Thessaloniki is 'Selanik', which is also the Turkish. A few buildings were built before WW2. Their idiosyncratic architectural features made them more decorative and individual than their newer neighbours.

One of the town's main streets is named after Fuat Babani (1918-1943), who was born in the district and was killed by the fascist occupiers of Albania in the village of Hoçisht close to Bilisht. His last words were: "Although the conqueror is larger and armed, the people are stronger and will regain their freedom". Sloping down from 'his' road, there was a park. In its lower section, we noticed a social centre with at least one café. Along its upper edge, there were some cast-iron shelters, looking like small band-stands, where men were congregating, chatting, and playing cards. The fragrance of grilled meat permeated the air.

We drove to the outskirts of Korçë, where we joined the road to Voskopojë, about twenty kilometres further west. The first half of this road ran through flattish farmland and was poorly surfaced. Beyond the village of Voskop, the road became better in quality, and it wound steadily upwards through attractive hilly, occasionally wooded, terrain to Voskopojë.

Now, little more than a scattered village surrounded by hills, Voskopojë ('Moschopolis') was once an important city in the Balkans. Wace and Thompson in their 1913 book *The Nomads of the Balkans*, wrote:

"Of the two Muskopole … was the larger and most renowned, for it was the great commercial centre for Central Albania and Upper Macedonia and its merchants had branch houses in Venice, Vienna and Buda-Pest, and like their kinsfolk beyond the Danube frequented the great fair of Leipzig."

I first became aware of the existence of Moschopolis in the 1980s when my friend in Belgrade, the late Vesna Korac, showed me an old book in Serbian about Moschopolis. Its grainy black and white, blurry, photographs of the Byzantine churches and various ruined buildings haunted me, and made me want to see the place. In its heyday (the late 17th and much of the 18th century), it had a large population of Vlach (aka Aromanian) speaking people, many of whom were also fluent in Greek. The Vlachs are a semi-nomadic people. They have settled homes (for example Metsovon in Greece and Voskopojë in Albania), but spend much of the year roaming around, pasturing their flocks. Winnifrith in his *The Vlachs: The History of a Balkan People* wrote of the Vlachs:

"In scattered pockets throughout the central Balkans are to be found small communities of people speaking a dialect derived from Latin."

Wace and Thompson defined the Vlachs as "members of a distinct race". They speak an Eastern Romance language, and are scattered all over the Balkans.

Apart from its great economic influence over a wide area of the Balkans and far beyond it, Voskopojë was a centre of culture and religion. Once, there had been twenty-four churches in the city as well as the Balkan's first printing press (outside of Istanbul). The city's decline began in the 1760s when Albanian Muslims attacked it. In 1788, it was razed by the

Albanian born Ali Pasha (1740-1822) of Tepelenë, the so-called 'Lion of Janina' (Ioannina in Greek).

When we arrived at Voskopojë, nothing hinted that a thriving city, once greater in size than Belgrade or Athens, had ever stood there. Without prior knowledge, it was impossible to imagine this. The road to our hotel, the Ana Maria, was unmade, rutted, and pot-holed, but by then such treacherous looking roads no longer worried us. We were greeted by a friendly couple. Our only common language was Modern Greek. I know a few words, but no grammar. Our hosts were fluent, having worked in Greece for several years.

Exhausted, we rested in our room before dinner. At about 8 pm, just before sunset, I heard bells tinkling outside. I stood on our balcony, and watched cows, some with cow-bells attached to leather neck collars, being led home by men and women with dogs. The cows were soon followed by a large flock of sheep and goats. The tinkling was occasionally interrupted by the shouts of the men and women, and barking of their dogs. It was a magical rustic scene.

Our balcony afforded a view of lovely hills. There were many new buildings, mostly holiday villas, dotted about on the alpine slopes. There were some new houses, which looked unattractive and too close to one another, being constructed right next door to our hotel. Beyond them, there was an old stone bridge with two circular arches. It carried a stony road over a rustling stream. Above the bridge, there was a small church with a veranda over its main western entrance. Higher up the hill, behind the church and flush with the hillside, I saw two bulky concrete frames, each surrounding a pair of large rusting metal double doors, rather like the entrances to enormous garages or warehouses.

We were the only people eating in our hotel's spacious dining room. We were offered *gici*, which our phrase book translated as 'piggy'. The grilled baby pork was delicious. The pork we ate in Albania was the tastiest that I have ever eaten. Our hosts hovered around us throughout the meal. We conversed with them, employing my long-disused (scanty) Modern Greek vocabulary and Albanian words, which we looked up in our inadequate phrasebook. Despite linguistic hurdles, we recognised that our hosts were a warm, hospitable couple.

Statue of Violeta Manushi ('Teto Ollga') at Tushemisht

Café at Pustec (Liqenas)

Logs stored on a balcony in Bilisht

Restored church in Pustec (Liqenas)

Korçë

Monday, 30th May 2016 Our hosts, Theodoraq and his wife Konstandina, greeted us warmly before serving us a hearty breakfast. It included *petulla*, an Albanian pancake. Looking like flattened Indian *puris*, but much chewier in texture, they are served with something sweet. That morning, it was home-made cherry jam, which contained whole, pitted, cooked cherries. To balance this, we ate some very salty kaçkavalli cheese. This was washed down with something that was often served to us at breakfasts: *mali çai* – Mountain Tea, an infusion made with flowers of Sideritis ('iron wort'; *Sideritis syriaca*).

In Korçë, we parked close to the bazaar area in Rruga Viktimat e 7 Shkurktit. This street, named in honour of the Victims of the 7th of February (nobody has yet told me their story), was lined on one side by blocks of flats and a variety of shops, and on the other side by large industrial buildings with plenty of windows, mostly containing broken glass. A small street led into a large market area, which consisted of many outdoor stalls as well as a pair of big indoor halls. The bazaar area was very clean, much tidier than many other city markets that I have seen. Vendors offered us samples of their wares to taste. Several olive sellers displayed a bewildering range of olives, which we tasted. We bought a variety from Berat, which had a similar taste to Greek Kalamata olives. In addition to 'black' olives, I noticed that some of the olives on offer (and others served to us elsewhere in Albania) had a dark brownish-green colour, almost but not quite black.

The spotless, almost clinically clean, spacious halls contained numerous food stalls. There were many dairy product sellers with hard cheeses piled high on their counters, tubs of softer cheeses, and plastic buckets filled with different types of *salce kosi*, some of which was stuffed into large hollowed-out red and green capsicums. *Salce kosi*, which is usually savoury, can also be sweetened It resembles closely in consistency and appearance, but not taste, the Guajarati strained yoghurt dessert *shrikhand*. There were also fruit and vegetable sellers both inside the halls and outside under canopies. Their wares looked deliciously fresh. The meat and fish stalls were odourless, a complete contrast to those which I have seen when visiting food bazaars elsewhere.

We looked at the stalls selling non-food items, hoping to find something that we could use at home that would remind us of Albania every day, for example clothes pegs, but we looked in vain. Just about every manufactured item in the bazaar was imported (often from Albania's erstwhile ally China). This was almost always the case with packaged foods and drinks, which were mostly imported from Italy.

After exploring the bazaar, we walked to a central square that was bounded on one side by buildings dating back from Communist times, and on the other side by far older buildings. Lopa pointed out a man walking around a traffic roundabout in the middle of the square. He had a darkish complexion with close-cropped hair, and was wearing a large camera on a long neck-strap. He was leading a large off-white, light golden-brown, bear on a chain. I suspect that he made money by taking pictures of people posing with the bear.

Dayrell-Hill (see above) wrote that in pre-WW2 Albania there were two kinds of gypsy. One lived in towns and undertook menial work such as cleaning, both domestic and municipal. Known as *jevg*, they also operated fairground attractions such as merry-go-rounds and Ferris wheels. The others were Romany wanderers who moved from place to place often selling things, like baskets, which they had made. These were known in Albanian as *arixhi*, leaders of bears. Angus Fraser wrote in his book *The Gypsies* that in the twelfth century Theodore Balsamon (died c. 1204) wrote about a passage in the Council of Trullo (692 AD, also known as 'The Quinisext Council'.) which threatened a six-year excommunication for any member of the Church who exploited the public by displaying bears or other animals for amusement or by telling fortunes. Those who did so, like our man in Korçë, were known in the seventh century as 'bearkeepers' and were clearly not too concerned about excommunication because they continue to go about their business today.

We entered a small bookshop next to a post office in the ground floor of a Communist era apartment block. It was on the corner, where a street named after Edith Durham (see above) met another named after Fan Noli (1882-1965). Noli was the prolific Albanian theologian, writer, scholar, and politician, who became Albania's Prime minister briefly in 1924. We bought what turned out to be a picturesque but fairly inaccurate Albanian map of an area of the country that we were planning to visit later. I managed to resist the temptation to buy a copy of Pettifer's *Blue Guide to Albania and Kosovo* translated into Albanian, which had been reduced in price by 70%.

When we crossed an open space to reach the older part of the city centre, we passed a well-dressed late middle-aged lady standing next to her 'pay to get weighed' scales decorated with a small outline map of Albania. She was chatting to a distinguished looking elderly man. I had the feeling that earlier in her life she had been employed in something far more sophisticated than weighing.

When we entered the old part of town, we saw the covered entrance to the Han of Elbasan, a traditional Ottoman travellers' inn (aka 'khan') that dated back to the early eighteenth century. Arranged around its central courtyard, the upper storey rooms opened out onto a gallery overlooking it, rather like the George Inn, the last surviving old coaching hostelry in London. When we visited the han, it was being restored.

Edward Lear slept in hans in Albania. His experiences of them were not always good. These excerpts from his *Journals of a Landscape Painter in the Balkans* illustrate some of the problems he encountered:

"In large towns, the khan is a three-sided building enclosed in a courtyard, and consisting of two floors, the lower a stable, the upper divided into chambers, opening into a wooden gallery which runs all round the building, and to which you ascend outside by stairs. ... Three khans did we explore in vain, their darkness and vermin being too appalling to overcome; luckily there was still a fourth ..."

And:

"O khan of Tyrana! rats, mice, cockroaches, and all lesser vermin were there. Huge flimsy cobwebs, hanging in festoons above my head; big frizzly moths, bustling into my eyes and fare, for the holes representing windows I could close but imperfectly with sacks and baggage ..."

The hans were not all bad. For example, between Elbasan and Tirana:

"There were whispering olives hanging over the khan-yard; and while a simple melody was chanted by three Gheghes in the shade, the warm, slumbrous midday halt brought back to memory many such scenes and siestas in Italy."

After reading Lear's comments, I wondered whether inns in Great Britain were likely to have been so much more hygienic than those in Albania in the late 1840s. When the han in Korçë, whose layout is exactly as Lear described above, is finally restored, it will be a wonderful place to visit and maybe even to stay in. Given the high standards of Albanian accommodation that we discovered, Lear would be pleasantly surprised were he able to revisit Albania now.

The street with the han was part of a warren of streets that made up the old bazaar area of the city. They were lined with old buildings, mostly well-restored compared with how they were when I visited Korçë in 1984. The heart of this area is a wide, open space surrounded by shops and cafés. While it was not exactly 'buzzing' with activity when we sat down to have a coffee there, it was far livelier than when I visited it one afternoon in May 1984. On that afternoon, all the shops were tightly closed with metal shutters, leading me to think that the area was due for demolition. Later, I will explain why I might have conceived that notion.

The old buildings of Korçë are mostly two-storeyed with tiled roofs. Most of them are attractive: some resembling those which we saw on the Pedonalja in Shkodër, but others with different appearances. Some of them would not have looked out of place in the Plaka district of Athens, which I used to visit in the 1960s and 1970s. Maybe, I thought this knowing of Greece's historical influence and interest in Korçë. In 1912, Greek forces occupied the city and held it until 1913. In the years that followed, Korçë was again occupied by the Greeks between 1916 and 1920. It became the capital of the 'Autonomous Albanian Republic of Korçë' created by French forces during WW1. Its police force was commanded by the locally-born Themistokli Gërmenji, who was executed in 1917 by the French after having been erroneously accused of collaborating with the Central Powers (Germany and its allies). After 1920, the city was restored to Albania. In 1936, the future dictator Enver Hoxha taught grammar at the French Lycée. Korçë today (and when I visited in 1984) gave the impression of being a more typically European city than most other cities in Albania except for Tirana. Oakley-Hill had the same impression when he visited it in the 1930s. He wrote:

"Korçë itself had a modern look and there was a wide central street containing the prefecture and other official buildings. From there, past the cathedral, a wide street led... This street might have been on the outskirts of any English town; it was tree-lined, and the rows of houses were detached, with front gardens..."

The cathedral was demolished (see below), and the street has changed somewhat, with most but not all the front gardens gone, but is still tree-lined. Amongst Albanians, the city has the reputation of being a centre of culture.

The Sheshi I Teatrit (Theatre Square) is an elongated open space pinched like an egg-timer. At one end, there is a bank, which was built by the Italians in the 1930s, and at the other the garish Grand Hotel Palace. This hotel was not yet built when I visited the city in 1984, but there was another in its place, the Hotel Turizm, which is where I stayed. The old, now demolished hotel, had a first-floor terrace with outdoor tables and chairs. It was from there that I took a picture of the old bank across the open space in 1984. Then, the bank had been a branch of the nationally owned State Bank of Albania, but now it is used by a privately owned Turkish bank. In 1984, a traffic policeman stood in a small white circle painted in the middle of the square. Even though he went through the motions of directing traffic, there was none.

We walked up the gently sloping, elegant, tree-lined pedestrianised Bulevari Shen Gjergi. At one end of it, white stones have been set in the pavement to show the outlines of the former St George Cathedral, which was demolished by Enver Hoxha's cronies in 1968. Near this, we saw a Communist war memorial dedicated to partisans from Korçë, and a gallery of art built during Communist times. Much of this boulevard is lined with elegant buildings that predate WW2. Halfway along the gently sloping thoroughfare we saw a building that made a great impression on me in 1984 because its architecture resembled turn of the century (end of nineteenth) Romanian architecture.

On our recent trip, I discovered that this building was marked on a map as the 'Romanian House'. A plaque beneath one of its balconies read: "T.T.I. 1928". This stands for "Tashko Tasi Ilo 1928". I believe that the history of this incongruous building, which is not mentioned in any of the many guidebooks (both Albanian and English) that I have consulted, is as follows. TT Ilo and his brother the writer Spyridon T Ilo (1876-1950) left their native Korçë for Bucharest in Romania at an early age. Cities in Romania, Bulgaria, Egypt, and Italy, were, wrote Stuart Mann in his *Albanian Literature*, centres where cultured (often literary) Albanians congregated. Many of them were involved in the drive for Albanian independence which gathered momentum at the beginning of the twentieth century. Spyridon was involved in the Albanian independence movement and was responsible for details in the design of the country's national flag, and, also, a signatory of the Albanian Declaration of Independence in 1912. In 1916, he moved to the USA, and seven years later he returned to Korçë. He founded a record company that made the first recordings of the Albanian National Anthem. In 1946, he 'donated' his recording studio to the city.

Tashko brought the newly written National Anthem from Romania to Albania. He and his wife Alexandra lived in the 'Romanian' house until they were evicted by the Communists because they supported the monarchy. Tashko died a broken man in 1964, his wife 20 years later. Knowing about the Ilo family, made sense of a Romanian-style building in Korçë. On its ground floor at the corner, where the main entrance must have once been, there is a minimarket which displays the Vodafone logo. The omnipresence this company's white and red logo's in today's Albania has replaced that of the Communist era's innumerable political slogans. Before 1991, they appeared everywhere: on buildings, alongside roads, and even on mountainsides.

At the upper end of the boulevard we found the recently constructed Orthodox cathedral, the Katedralja Ngjallja e Krishtit (Resurrection of Christ Cathedral), which was completed in the early 1990s. Bustling with tiled domes and hemi-domes and flanked by two elaborate bell towers, this huge edifice looked like an oversized elaborate wedding cake. Its interior was attractive, but not overly so.

Although the National Mediaeval Art Museum was only a short distance east of the new cathedral, we had difficulty finding it. We asked several people for directions. We only found it when we were led there by an Orthodox priest with a beard and black robes. He was going in that direction because his destination was a smartly restored nineteenth century mansion opposite the museum. The building he entered, the Metropolitan of Korçë, had a plaque with some indistinct letters in Greek above the door. It was dated 12th June 1896, ten days after the city had suffered a great earthquake. But, this is not why the plaque had been placed there. It commemorated the men who financed a new building for the Metropolitan after the old one had been destroyed a fire caused by an unknown arsonist in 1896.

Surrounded by old houses, the museum's façade looked like a nondescript office block. When I visited it in 1984, it was as well-guarded as a national bank or an important ministry. When we entered the shabby foyer in 2016, the place looked closed and deserted. Eventually, a man and a woman appeared from an upper floor, and opened an electrically operated steel shutter to reveal the entrance to the museum itself.

They explained to us that the museum had once been a church. It had been 'disguised' by the Communists by replacing its ecclesiastical façade with its present ugly secular one. The layout of the museum resembled that of a church. The museum was a treasure house of icons. It contained some of the best examples of those church paintings that had survived the mass-destruction of theological objects and buildings during Hoxha's 'Cultural Revolution' when religion was banned in Albania. Fortunately, several thousand of the best examples of Albanian religious paintings were deemed to have had too much cultural value to have been destroyed. These were saved, and hidden from the Albanian public in stores and closely guarded museums. As for the rest, the major part of Albania's religious heritage was callously demolished.

The museum contained a display of icons, which are both magnificent and varied. If I had to choose only one museum to visit in Albania, this would be it. The 'stars' of this uniformly superb collection are the icons painted by the sixteenth century Albanian painter Onufri (Onouphrios of Neokastro, from Elbasan), and by his sons. Onufri was particularly active in Venice and Berat. Many of his paintings contain a particularly bright red pigment, which helps make his Italianate icons recognisable.

As in a church, the museum consisted of a central aisle or nave flanked by two side aisles that ran beneath raised wooden galleries. Half way up the stairs to one of these galleries, we stopped to look at a depiction of St Christopher with the head of a dog. The two custodians, who spoke good English, told us the story. Apparently, St Christopher, to his distress, was very attractive to women. He used to ferry people across a river. One day, he had a small child on his back. The child got increasingly heavier as Christopher waded across the river. He asked the child, who happened to be Jesus, what was happening. He told Christopher (his name is from the Greek words meaning 'carrier of Christ') that he was carrying all the sins of the world. Christopher, who wanted to become less attractive for reasons of piety, asked Jesus to help him. Jesus obliged by giving the saint's head the appearance of a dog. This is an example of cynocephaly, meaning 'having the head of a dog'. The Byzantines began representing St Christopher that way during the reign of Emperor Diocletian in the 3rd century AD.

After exploring the museum, which has, since our visit, moved to newly built premises, we looked at its northern external side wall, which retained some features of the original church. The curators in the museum pointed out that a part of the building housing the museum was being used as a church. We saw its entrance next to the outer entrance to the museum building. Because it had pictures of icons displayed on either side of its door I had at first thought that it was an advertisement for the museum rather than the entrance of a church.

Back on the pedestrianised St Georges Boulevard, we saw a ruined shell of a building, consisting only of its outer walls. A notice on the fence surrounding it, written in both Albanian and Greek and having the Greek flag printed on it, informed that these remains had been the Greek consulate before WW2. This was one of the only buildings still to have a front garden, such as Oakley-Hill described above. Between 1936 and

1938, the consul was the already noted Greek poet/diplomat George Seferi (1900-1971). In an interview conducted in 1968 and published in the *Paris Review* (issue 50, 1970), the aged diplomat said of Korçë:

"A very good place for me for writing was when I was in Albania because I was quite unknown there, and very isolated; at the same time I was near Greece, I mean, from the language point of view, and I could use my free time to advantage. There were no exhausting social functions."

We ate lunch in the lovely gardens of the neighbouring building, a restaurant called "Vila Themistokli", housed in Themistokli Gërmenji's former home (also retaining its front garden). Although portions were small by Albanian standards, the food was good. My *qofta* were flavoured with a hint of dill, a much-used herb in Albania. Lopa enjoyed a spicy spinach soup that contained tiny *qofta* flavoured with mint. I washed down my meal with tasty chilled locally-brewed Korça brand beer. According to the label on the bottle, this brew won "Grand Prix hors concours" in Thessaloniki both in 1936 and 1938. The brewery was started in 1929 by the Italian Umberto Umberti and the Albanian Selim Mboria. During the Communist years, it was nationalised, but now it is back in private hands.

During the hottest part of the afternoon, we tried to visit the city's oldest mosque, the Xhamia e Mirahorit. We knew it was close by, we saw the top of its minaret, but could not discover how to reach it. Near the Town Hall, we asked a teenage girl, who, instead of pointing out where it was, kindly offered to lead us there. We set off in what seemed to be in the wrong direction, but whenever we tried to check that she had understood where we wanted to go, she replied: "Lezzgo" (i.e. let's go). Lopa had a bad ankle, and walking was becoming painful for her. I tried to explain this to our guide, but all she did was to turn around to Lopa, who was lagging behind, saying: "Come on. Lezzgo." There was no stopping this keen youngster. She led us further and further away from the city centre into a suburb consisting of shabby Communist period apartment blocks, all the time exhorting us with "lezzgo." After a while, she pointed to a distant minaret, and indicated that we had arrived. We walked where she had pointed, and arrived at a very grand looking mosque. However, it had been built in 2011 by the modern Turks, rather than by their Ottoman ancestors. It was a fine building with a lovely, airy, delicately decorated interior, but it was not what we had been looking for.

Weary and hot, we tried to retrace our steps back into the centre. Quite by chance, we began walking along a road that led straight to the Mirahorit Mosque, which was closed when we arrived. However, some men were gathering outside it, and soon the imam arrived to unlock it for afternoon *namaaz* (prayers). They were all friendly and welcoming. While we were waiting, we were joined by a German lady, who was keen to see this mosque that dated back to 1496. Restored by a Turkish organisation in 2014, it was worth waiting to enter it. The interior was decorated with attractive frescoes depicting various mosques and Muslim pilgrimage places including the Kaaba. One of the men who was waiting with us to enter the mosque asked Lopa where she was from. When she said India, he exclaimed "Rye Kapur", that being his pronunciation of Raj Kapoor, a well-known Bollywood film star. As we had already discovered in Pukë, Bollywood is popular in Albania.

The German lady asked whether she could join us because she had been in Korçë for a month, and felt deprived of conversation because she spoke no Albanian. We decided to find a café, but at 4 pm in Korçë, this was not an easy thing to do. The centre of the city was almost dead. It had become an urban 'Marie-Celeste'. Most shops were tightly shuttered up just as they had been when I visited the city one afternoon in 1984. The city closed-down in the afternoon. We found an unattractive café. Its owner detached himself from his group of cronies, and reluctantly served us coffees.

The German, Luisa, an artist, was spending a month with a holy order, helping children to paint. Though she had been given hospitality by the nuns, they were far too busy to chat with her, so we must have seemed a godsend. While we drank, we watched a couple of drunks staggering around in the street, and saw several policemen. There was no one else around. The café owner made it obvious that he did not want us hanging around chatting for too long, so we said goodbye to Luisa, and returned to our car.

At the hamlet of Turan-i-Sipërme between Korçë and Voskop, we left the main road at to examine a solitary tall old tower with gothic windows. It might have once been part of a church or maybe a watch-tower.

We drove through Voskop, and then up into the heart of Voskopojë, which we had not yet explored. In the middle of the village's central square we saw a monument commemorating the 28th of December 1943. Raised on a podium, it consisted of a tall column, topped with a five-pointed star, next to a wall with six long lists of names. Those on the list were 'martyred' members of the 4th Assault Brigade, founded on the date on the monument. They liberated large areas of territory around Korçë from the Germans.

We visited the nearby church of Shën Koll (St Nicholas), the best-preserved church in the town. Fortunately, it was unlocked, and its priest showed us around. A cloister-like veranda (or loggia) ran along the church's southern side. This contained a few frescoes, mostly depictions of saints. Some of the pictures had been damaged in places by people scratching their names in the plaster. The interior of this lovely church was awash with frescoes, which we were not permitted to photograph. The iconostasis and delicately carved wooden pulpit and ceremonial throne were lovely. Some of the icons from the iconostasis are now in the museum that we visited in Korçë.

The priest told us that he is a Vlach, and speaks the Vlach language. Many inhabitants of Voskopojë, including our hosts Theodoraq and Konstandina, are Vlachs, who still speak their own language (as well as many others). After seeing this church, we drove along a particularly treacherous track to see another church, the Fjeta e Shen Marise, a cathedral dedicated to the dormition of St Mary. It was closed, but by peering over its enclosing wall I could see a couple of frescoes decorating arches open to the elements.

We returned to the Ana Maria for a second evening meal of delicious grilled *gici* with a good salad, and raki. Before dinner, as on the evening before, I stood on our balcony watching the cows with bells being herded along the road outside our hotel.

Cattle at Voskopojë

Olive seller in market at Korçë.

Romanian style house in central Korçë

Bear and keeper in Korçë. Note buildings in old city centre in the background.

Dardhë, Mborje, Voskop

Tuesday, 31st May 2016 We had been recommended to visit Dardhë, a village south of Korçë. To reach it, we drove from Korçë along the main road leading to Ersekë. This was appalling because its tarmac had been removed in anticipation of resurfacing. We drove along it at snail's pace, bumping constantly on an uneven expanse of sharp rocks, and raising clouds of white dust like thick smoke. After a while, we joined a smaller but properly surfaced side-road that led across the plain through the village of Boboshticë. Then, we climbed through a wild, barren rocky landscape. Gradually the road began ascending ever more steeply and curling around sharp hairpin bends until we crossed the top of a pass.

Then, we descended through a well-forested mountainous landscape. Dardhë clings to the slopes of these hills, and overlooks a cultivated plain far below.

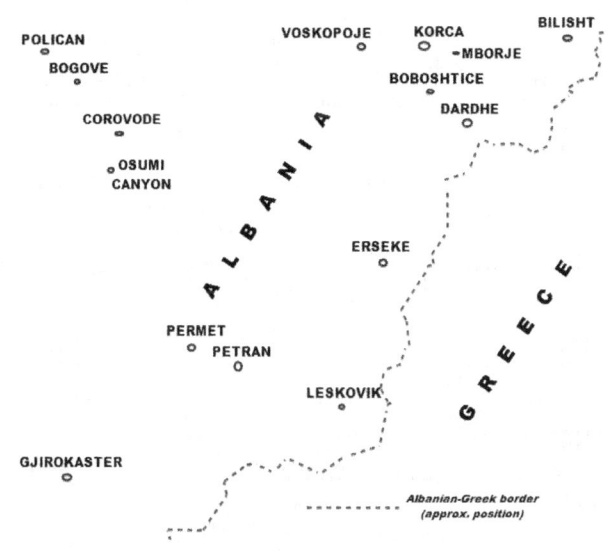

Map showing approximate positions of some places visited in southern Albania (central and eastern parts)

We parked our car beside a stone building, dated 1936. It had a newish sign indicating that it is the *Pleqesia* (presbytery) of Dardhë. We entered a small steeply sloping park full of shady trees. Inside the park, there was a building that houses a museum (the Muzeu Foto-Historik), which was closed. The headstone of the arch of the museum's main entrance bore the date 1924. Below it, there was a plaque, which recorded that the building had been constructed with assistance from members of the Dardhë society, named "BLETA", whose members resided in the USA. After returning to the UK, I contacted BLETA, which still exists and has its headquarters in Worcester (Massachusetts). I learned that the present-day museum was originally a school. Many inhabitants from Dardhë emigrated to the USA. Their families formed the nuclei of the first Albanian communities both in the USA and in Romania. One of these migrants from Dardhë was Josif Pani (1868-1934), who was deeply involved in important American Albanian patriotic groups, notably Vatra (meaning 'hearth'), whose members included prominent Albanians such as the influential writer Faik Konitza (1875-1942) and former Prime Minister Fan Noli.

Another plaque on the building, cracked in one corner, was topped with a five-pointed star. It dated back to Communist times, and read (translated): "Important international meetings concerning the regional character of the province were held in this building during the national liberation war. It was the centre of partisan forces and warehouse for food and propaganda materials."

Dardhë is mentioned in Roderick Bailey's book about the SOE in Albania, *The Wildest Province*. When the village fell into German hands, its terrified inhabitants appeared to welcome them. Various members of the SOE recorded having spent time in the place. Bailey wrote that Major Peter Kemp (1913-1993) recorded that the villagers were "Catholics", and that two of his fellow 'Britishers' had attended mass in a church "above Dardhë". As the church in the centre of Dardhë is Orthodox, Kemp must have been referring to Shën Pjeter, which is in the hills above the village. On our way to Dardhë, we had stopped briefly at a point above it, where we spotted a roadside shrine dedicated to St Peter. It bore a Roman Catholic (rather than Orthodox) cross. Kemp's obituary in the *Guardian* newspaper (4th November 1993) noted that:

"He spent 10 months clandestinely in Albania, many of them in disagreeable proximity to Enver Hoxha, the Communist leader. He had several close brushes with death, and found the complexities of Balkan politics intensely confusing in a many-sided war."

In the park, there was a war memorial: a bust of a man wearing a neck scarf (like those worn by Communist 'young pioneers') and on his head, something resembling an Indian 'Nehru cap'. It commemorated partisans fallen in WW2. An embossed metal plate listed the dead. They died on various dates between 24th December 1942 and 20th August 1944. More than half of the seventeen listed died on the 9th of September 1943. All of them were born in Dardhë and were described as 'rene deshmor', meaning 'martyred'. On the 24th December 1942, Dardhë was attacked by Italian forces. On the 9th of September, a year later, the date on the memorial, their forces left the village, sacking it before doing so.

We visited the attractive Orthodox church of St George, close to the museum. It was being restored. The BLETA organisation has been assisting this. There was scaffolding on its bell-tower. Many of its fittings, including a lovely iconostasis and two intricate chandeliers made with gold coloured double-headed eagles, were of recent manufacture. An elaborately carved wooden icon stand looked older.

I wandered around the village, looking at its old stone houses that clung to the steep slopes of the mountainside. Their roofs were tiled with overlapping flat stones that resembled thick slates. There was a stone arch over the gateway to a drive that led to a building near where we had parked. The stonework on the side of the arch that faced inwards had a five-pointed star embedded in its headstone. The side of the arch facing the street no longer had one.

We had drinks in a modern hotel above the village. It resembled a large alpine chalet. We were the only customers in its vast comfortable bar. Although Dardhë was a pretty place and interesting, it failed to impress me as much as it had the person who had recommended it. However, the wild scenery along the way there and back made the detour worth making.

On our way to the village of Mborje on the eastern edge of Korçë, we stopped by a Communist war memorial at Boboshticë. It stated that the village had been a base of the National Liberation Army, and that on the 3rd of April 1943 it had been "burned and massacred" by 'Nazi-fascist collaborator's. Memorials such as these constantly reminded us of the horrors that the delightful Albanians had to suffer before they were subjected to the terrors inflicted, supposedly in their name, by Enver Hoxha and his accomplices.

In Drenovë, we saw a bust of the poet Aleksander Drenova (1872-1947), who wrote the words of *Hymni i Flamurit*, Albania's national anthem. The words of this were first published in an Albanian newspaper printed in Bulgaria in April 1912, and set to a tune adapted from a work by the Romanian composer Ciprian Porumbescu (1853-1883). Drenova, also known as 'Asdreni', was born in Drenovë and in 1885 moved to Bucharest (where he died). There, he became involved with Romania's Albanian community, whose members included the Ilo family (mentioned above).

At Mborje, we found a small mosque. Its minaret had a much greater diameter than most others we saw in Albania. It was topped with an attractive balustrade. On the whole, the minarets of the mosques in Albania, usually recently built, had tall slender minarets that looked from a distance like missiles or rockets. Some of them were so slim that it looked impossible for anyone to climb within them. The newer minarets were probably designed this way because the muezzin's call is now usually made through a loudspeaker. The minaret at Mborje was wide enough for even a well-fed muezzin to ascend to its balcony to call the faithful to prayer.

The main attraction of Mborje is its tiny Byzantine Church of the Holy Resurrection. This was just about visible through the scaffolding covering it. Unfortunately, it was locked up. This was a shame because it is said to contain wonderful frescoes. Small patches of the church's elaborately patterned exterior brickwork were scorched where pious visitors had lit prayer candles presumably because they too were unable to enter the locked building.

After viewing what we could of the church's exterior, we found a nearby 'taverna', the Bar Grill Ristozi, where we ate lunch. As in so many places where we ate or drank in Albania, there was a television turned on without sound. Greek popular music was being played through the restaurant's hi-fi loudspeakers. Several potted plants were being trained to grow up along tall fluorescent lighting tubes stuck into the soil. The owner, a member of Albania's Greek-speaking minority, offered us the choice of a menu either in Greek or in Albanian. We had a good meal that included excellent pork kebabs. We thought that we were eating late at 2 pm, but it was not until about thirty minutes later that the restaurant began to fill up.

Between the outskirts of Korçë and Drenovë the cultivated countryside was dotted with disused, derelict buildings. They looked as if they had been built during the Communist period for either industrial or administrative uses. Much of the Korça Beer brewery resembled these derelict structures, but we noticed there was modern section, where this refreshing drink is still being made. Next to the brewery, there was a beer garden, which was almost opposite the city of Korçë's large regional hospital.

When we stopped for coffee in a café in Voskop, an agricultural village with a mosque, on the way back up to Voskopojë, we were served by its Albanian Greek owner. On reaching Voskopojë, we tried to find one of the town's ruined churches by following a sign that pointed towards it. After a while, the terribly surfaced road divided into two unmarked grassy tracks, both totally unsuitable for our car. I asked a couple of farming types where the church was. They pointed at a clump of trees that partially hid a pile of stones that looked indistinguishable from builders' waste. I am not sure that was what we were searching for.

On arrival at the Ana Maria I took a walk to look at the concrete bunker entrances that we could see from our balcony. Surrounded by hefty, thick concrete frames, each of the entrances had pairs of metal doors locked closed with padlocks. These doors sealed an entrance large enough to admit the biggest of trucks. However, I saw no track approaching these entrances into the nearly vertical face of the hill. Maybe, there had been one in the past. Theodoraq told me that these doors had been the entrances to tunnels in the hillside that housed tanks and other military equipment. In addition to bunkers, Enver Hoxha had ordered the building of underground tunnels for housing military hardware and personnel to keep them out of sight of enemy aeroplanes and troops.

Hoxha was concerned about the risks of invasion. Even though he declared, "When the enemy attacks you, it means you are on the right road", he wanted to be prepared for when the attack began. Soon after his regime had gained control of Albania, there were at least two attempts to land or drop troops to try to topple it. The CIA in league with MI6 made these attempts in the period between 1949 and 1953. In his autobiography, *My Silent War*, Philby wrote of the infiltrations:

"The operation, of course, was futile from the beginning. Our infiltrators could achieve something only by penetrating the towns, which were firmly under Communist control."

It was also 'futile', because the Albanians knew about the plans because of information 'leaked' in advance by Kim Philby, the double-agent. He did not mention this in his autobiography.

Apart from these attempted attacks, Hoxha was sensible to be wary as his country was surrounded by neighbours who had long coveted Albanian territory. In addition to hostile neighbours, there was always the risk that the country might be attacked using nuclear weapons. I wondered how long Albania with all its concrete defence-work would have resisted hostile forces.

We ate dinner in the centre of Voskopojë at the Bardhe Brothers' restaurant close to the large WW2 monument. Its owners were Vlachs. After dinner, we returned to our hotel and sat with Konstandina and Theodoraq, drinking *raki mani* (mulberry raki), which had been made in Drenovë, where Theodoraq was born.

Tower at Turan-i-Sipërme, just west of Korçë on the road to Voskopojë

Many Albanians ride side-saddle. This picture was taken at Voskopojë.

Minaret at Mborje, near Korçë. Unlike newer minarets in Albania, this one is of a sufficient diameter for a man to climb within it.

To Gjirokastër

Wednesday, 1st June 2016 As the crow flies, Gjirokastër is about sixty kilometres southwest of Voskopojë. By car, it is over two hundred kilometres, because the roads that connect the two places skirt around the edges of parallel ranges of mountains running approximately north to south across the southern half of Albania. Before departing Voskopojë, our hosts Konstandina and Theodoraq hugged us affectionately, and then wished us "*kalo taxidhi*", the Greek for 'bon voyage'.

Our long journey along route SH 75 began at the western industrial edge of Korçë. We had been on this road on our way to Dardhë, and knew that we would have to make our way painfully slowly along the section of it that was under repair. We had no idea how much of the road was going to be so awful, and prayed that it would improve before long. We crawled along the first fifteen kilometres of the road, never exceeding fifteen kilometres per hour. Then, the road's surface improved considerably, but driving remained challenging because of the mountainous nature of the territory through which we travelled. For about five hours, we wound through the magnificent mountainous terrain that separates Albania from Greece.

We kept catching sight of high mountains with black summits streaked with snow. Endlessly changing breath-taking vistas of craggy peaks and verdant valleys greeted us as we drove slowly along the sinuous SH 75. When Oakley-Hill travelled along it in the 1930's, he rated it as "… the good road south to Ersekë". Marked as a main road on our detailed map, this thoroughfare was hardly broader than an English country lane, and not one of the better roads in present day Albania. Luckily, there was little traffic on it. Occasionally, we stopped to allow farm animals and their guardians, human and canine, to pass us. For almost half of our journey, our road was never further than twenty kilometres from the Greek border that runs along the peaks and ridges of the mountains of Epirus including Mount Grammos. Sometimes, we were within less than five kilometres of the mountainous frontier. Near Ersekë, we saw a road leading off to Bezhan, an Albanian village only two kilometres from Greece as the crow flies, but separated from the neighbouring country by forbiddingly steep high mountain slopes.

Our arrival in the small town of Ersekë, one of the highest towns in Albania (1050 metres), at about 11.30 am coincided with the emergence of a crowd of schoolchildren from a school in the town centre. It seemed too early for school to be adjourning for lunch. Most of the buildings surrounding the large grassy Parku Rinia (Youth Park), date back to Communist times. At one corner of the park, the we saw a monument to the partisans, bearing the date "20 Tetor 1944" (20th October 1944). It celebrated the liberation from German occupiers of the town and its surroundings by the Second Brigade of Ersekë.

Onwards through the mountains we went, encountering more flocks of animals and passing the occasional Cold War concrete bunkers in varying states of disrepair. In one tiny village, we saw an impressive sculptural WW2 memorial. It consisted of a grim-faced partisan resting his hand on the shoulder of an equally grim-faced girl. His right foot rested on the top of a German army helmet lying on the ground.

At lunchtime, we stopped at the Vila Germenji Jorgo Hotel in the forested mountains between Ersekë and Leskovik. The dining room looked out over a garden, which contained several rows of grape-vines. I ordered *tava kosi*. What arrived looked unappealing, but tasted good. A traditional Albanian dish, it consisted of chunks of lamb baked in yoghurt and rice. The restaurant was owned by Mr Guci, a graduate of the University of Korçë. Apart from running his establishment, he is also a sculptor. Two of his creations, which were made from parts from machines (springs, cog-wheels, and so on) painted in different colours were on display outside his restaurant. He described them as being 'abstracts'. I liked them.

Having eaten, we continued moving in a south-west direction, always hugging the Greek border. As we drove towards Leskovik, we were surrounded by yet more magnificent high mountains covered with patches of snow. 'Breathtakingly beautiful' is a cliché, but it was appropriate to describe the landscape. Surrounded by mountains, Leskovik, through which we drove, contained Communist era apartment buildings and two enormous hemispherical concrete bunkers close to each other. Both had rings of grass growing around them like cleric's tonsures.

Halfway along the meandering road between Leskovik and Çarçovë, we entered Gjirokastër County. On the county border, we saw goats grazing on both sides of the road. At Çarçovë, which we reached through a narrow pass (almost a ravine), there was a T-junction. The left turn led to Greece. We turned right, and began heading north-west, after having travelled in a south westerly direction since leaving Korçë. Suddenly, the weather transformed itself: rain and clouds yielded to hot sunshine.

We began following the valley of the River Vjosa (in Greek: Αώος). Rising in Greece, it flows through eighty kilometres of that country before entering Albania. It enters the Adriatic north of Vlorë, having passed through Përmet and Tepelenë, the birthplace of wily Ali Pasha, who entertained Lord Byron as his guest in 1809.

The water in the Vjosa was a rich turquoise colour. We stopped in the village of Petran at a café called Alvi, which had tables on a terrace overlooking the river. Upstream, we saw people standing on the sandy river bank washing their laundry in the water. Downstream, a narrow suspension bridge crossed the Vjosa. We stepped onto its swaying walkway, which was made of wooden planks to which wooden speed breakers had been attached at regular intervals. Opposite the café, I noticed a building with three rusty steel concrete reinforcement rods protruding from its flat roof. A ram's or goat's skull with elegantly curved horns was wedged amongst them. This was to ward off the 'evil-eye' (*syri i keq* in Albanian) Some Albanians told me that animal horns, rather than whole skulls, are often incorporated in a new building for good luck.

The country's hero Gjergj Kastrioti ('Skanderbeg') had a goat's skull complete with horns atop his helmet (which now resides in the Collection of Arms and Armour at the Neue Burg in Vienna). After he conquered Egypt, Alexander the Great was known by the Arabs as "Iskander Dhu l-Karnejn" (Arabic for: Alexander, the two horned) when he styled himself "Son of Ammon" (the god Ammon, who was worshipped in ancient Macedonia where Alexander was born, is often depicted wearing rams' horns). Kastrioti adopted the name Skanderbeg (Lord Alexander), which comes from 'Iskender' and 'bey', being Turkish for 'Alexander' and 'Lord' respectively.

The paving in the central square of Përmet was undergoing extensive renovation. We parked beside the clinic of a microbiologist/'biopathologist' with a Greek name. She had studied both at the hospital of Ioannina and at London's Royal Free. During Enver Hoxha's time, the only foreign trained doctors allowed to work in Albania were the very few whom the dictator trusted enough to give him treatment. Across the road, a large restored building bore a new plaque that read (in translation): "September 13, 1943 the day of liberation of Përmet from the Nazi invaders". This was accompanied by a flag crossed with a rifle, but not the five-pointed star of Communism.

After visiting a tourist office in the brand new cultural centre, we picked our way through the construction works in the city's square to reach an impressive monument. It celebrated the Congress of Përmet, which was held in the town in May 1944 when the Germans' defeat began to look likely. Then, the question of who was going to govern liberated Albania became important. The British and Americans, who had helped the Communist partisans in Albania, were against post-war Communist rule in the country. The Communist-dominated National Liberation Front of Albania held the congress in to ensure that Albania did not fall under the political influence of the Western Allies. Stefanaq Pollo and Arben Puto wrote in their *The History of Albania*, published in Tirana in 1981:

"On the basis of the report submitted by Enver Hoxha, the Congress took the historical decision 'to set a new democratic Albania for the people'."

In the words of a guidebook published in Albania in 1969:

"It was in Përmet that the Anti-Fascist National-liberation Congress met on May 24,1944 ..., and elected the General Anti-Fascist National-liberation Council, with the attributes of a Provisional Government, and where a whole series of important decisions were taken, among which that of barring the return of Ahmet Zogu to Albania and that of cancelling the old treaties concluded to the detriment of the Albanian people."

By May 1944, the Communists in the guise of the National Liberation Front had effectively won the civil war that had been raging in Albania at the same time as the Axis forces were being repelled. The same thing had been happening in Yugoslavia, leading to Tito and his Communist followers assuming government, and in Greece where the Communists failed in to gain control.

Near the monument, we saw a run-down building that had once been a cinema. A bust of Naim Frasheri (1845-1900) stood near it. He was a well-regarded Albanian poet and a member of Rilindja Kombëtare (The National Awakening), a group of prominent Albanian nationalists who campaigned for their country's independence. The cinema's windows were mostly bricked up or damaged. Part of the veranda surrounding the ground floor had been filled with a ramshackle structure made of wooden boards, some covered with plastic sheeting. A few icons were hanging outside this makeshift construction, an Orthodox church. Its interior was simple: icons, iconostasis, and a few pews.

On the edge of a park with tall trees close to the cinema, there was a tall shiny black stone monument bearing the date 9th March 1997. It commemorated six innocent citizens of Përmet who were executed by government forces during the great unrest – actually, a civil war – following the collapse of Albania's pyramid investment schemes in 1997. These, which were allegedly set up with governmental collusion, offered

Albania's then financially naïve population unrealistically large returns for investments.

An excellent road connected Përmet to the lower (newer) part of the city of Gjirokastër. We had no idea of the exact location of our B&B, but knew that it was in the upper, older part of the city. Before long, we were driving up extremely steep cobbled streets. Occasionally, I had to reverse to let other cars pass, and then had to make tricky hill starts. It was pure luck that we spotted the Kotoni B&B quickly because navigating the old city in a car would have been very tricky. This family run establishment is in one of the many old patrician dwellings that make the city so attractive. The owner's brother welcomed us, and then served us coffee and raki. He spoke German because he had worked in Germany for a while, and a little Greek. His sister, the owner, spoke Italian.

The views from our accommodation were superb. High above, loomed the walls of the town's large castle. The clock tower in the castle had circular clock faces with Roman numerals. I wondered if these were the clocks removed from Paget's tower in Shkodër. In another direction, the grey tiled roofs of the bazaar of old Gjirokastër spread out below us. And elsewhere, we saw serried ranks of mountains on either side of the wide valley of the River Drinos.

We dined in Rruga Gjon Bue. We ordered 'biftek', expecting beef steak, but we were served grilled pork instead. After an unexceptional meal, we entered the café beneath the Bazaar Mosque. The young waiter had difficulty understanding us, but a man, who spoke good English because he had worked in London, helped us. Sitting near us, he began telling us a series of things about Albania, which might have been 'coffee house gossip' without much truth. He seemed to enjoy conspiracy theories. Because of my reservations about the reliability of what he told us, I will not reveal what he said about the Prime Minister's father, a colleague of Enver Hoxha's Communist successor Ramiz Alia. Also, I give little credence to his statement that Enver Hoxha ever met Queen Elizabeth II.

To digress a little, the nearest thing to an association with the Queen was that Mehmet Shehu had travelled to the UN in New York on the Queen Elizabeth liner in 1960. Shehu's transatlantic crossing might have been held against him later. Enver Hoxha, who was no stranger to re-writing history, wrote in his *The Titoites*, published a year after Shehu's mysterious death:

"At this time Mehmet Shehu was sent to New York at the head of a government delegation to the UNO. He travelled on the British trans-Atlantic luxury liner "Queen Elizabeth". We knew that Tito, also, was travelling on that ship, but it never crossed our minds that Mehmet Shehu might meet Tito. Now we learn from his fellow-travellers who were his collaborators and are now in jail that Harry Fultz of the American CIA and Randolph Churchill, who was an Intelligence Service agent but figured on the passenger list as a journalist, were also aboard. During this trip of seven days, Mehmet Shehu, being their agent, had secret meetings and talks with Tito, Fultz, and R. Churchill, informed them of the situation in and the stands of our Party…"

Our new acquaintance believed that the British warships, which were sunk in the Corfu Channel in the late 1940s, were destroyed by the British, rather than sunk by Albanian mines (as is commonly believed). He claimed that the British destroyed their own vessels deliberately, and then blamed the Albanians so that they could hang on to the Bank of Albania's large stash of gold bullion that had been rescued from the Germans after WW2 and then stored in London.

The chatty man in the coffee-house was from the village of Lazarat, a few kilometres south of Gjirokastër. This place, he said, had been one of the first to rebel against Enver Hoxha. It was also a centre for the cultivation of cannabis. In 2014, the police swooped on the place, burned the crop, and destroyed much of the village. He suggested that the present socialist government had been exceedingly tough with his village, which was not the only one where cannabis was grown, because it contained many opponents of socialism, past and present. The historian (and guidebook writer) Julian Pettifer, wrote that many of the people of Lazarat were opposed to socialism, both during and after the Communist period.

Between Korçë and Ersekë. Greece lies beyond the snow-capped mountains.

WW2 monument between Ersekë and Gërmenj

Makeshift church in an old cinema in Përmet.

Rams horns to ward off the 'evil eye', at Petran.

Gjirokastër

Thursday 2nd June 2016 Breakfast at the Kotoni was served in a ground-floor room decorated to look like a typical Ottoman reception room. Such rooms, which would have traditionally been located on an upper storey, had an elaborately carved wooden ceiling and a traditional fireplace under a moulded plaster canopy shaped like an inverted cone. A filling breakfast was served with delicately flavoured Mountain Tea.

The Kotoni was the first privately owned accommodation to be opened in Gjirokastër after Communism ended in 1990. It was named after the Kotoni family, who used to own this large house which was three hundred years old (like many of the other buildings in old Gjirokastër). Its distinctive white-painted façade with three triangular roof gables projecting over the street was visible from many points in the old city. The Kotoni family was allied with Ali Pasha from Tepelenë. During the Hoxha era, the family was evicted and forced to live in cramped conditions with two other families in only two rooms. The last surviving members of the family now live in Austria.

While the Kotoni family might have lost their ancestral home, the opposite is true of the Skenduli family, one of whose surviving members maintains the house owned almost continuously by his family since it was built. To reach the Skenduli House, we passed the front of a large high school, the Gjimnazi 'Asim Zeneli'. Founded in 1923, it was one of the first secondary schools in Albania, where students could enrol regardless of their gender, religion, and place of origin. Two famous Albanian writers, Dritero Agolli (born in Korçë) and Ismail Kadare (born in Gjirokastër), attended it. The road on which the school stands is named in honour of Kadare. Outside the school, we saw a dramatic bas-relief, bearing the information that on the 6th March 1942 the school's students and teachers clashed with the forces of fascism. They were protesting against the Italian occupation. Michael

Harrison on his informative website (www.michaelharrison.org.uk) noted that its artist included a double-headed eagle on the bas-relief, but omitted the five-pointed star of Communism. Where it ought to have been was covered by the arm of one of heroic students. Harrison commented that not all of the artists who made monuments for the regime were completely committed to it.

The Skenduli House stands almost opposite the high school. A sprightly middle-aged lady working on her roof noticed us, climbed down rapidly, and led us through the main entrance into its courtyard, where she had a table with souvenirs for sale. While we were examining her wares, we were greeted by an elderly man, Mr Skenduli - a member of the ninth generation of the family, who constructed the house in the eighteenth century.

He pointed out the large number of windows and chimneys on his house, telling us that these signified the family's great wealth and importance. There were remains of frescoes depicting animals, including the regal lion, painted underneath the roof's overhanging eaves. With great charm, Mr Skenduli showed us around the house, explaining things to us clearly in French.

The building was well fortified. On the ground and first floors, we saw numerous small slits in the thick stone walls. These were used for firing guns at unwelcome intruders. Like an Englishman's, an Albanian's home "is his castle". The lowest level of the building was used, amongst other things, for housing animals. A large door admitted them into the building. An external stone staircase led from the courtyard to the main entrance of the house on the floor above the lowest storey.

This floor with its tiny windows and firing-slits served as winter quarters. Mr Skenduli pointed out that the thick walls of the building, like those of many other buildings that we saw, consisted of layers of bricks and mortar separated at intervals by layers of a hard, but elastic timber. He explained that the wood protected the walls by absorbing shocks during seismic activity. The cement between the flagstones covering the floors of the winter quarters had always been painted red (the colour of Skanderbeg's flag), and was when we saw it. This was a sign of the family's Albanian patriotism even when they were also loyal Ottoman subjects.

The summer quarters were on the upper floors of the house. With large windows that offered splendid views of the city and surrounding mountains, these airy rooms were more ornate than those on the lower floors. Mr Skenduli pointed out the pipework in the overhanging eaves of the roof. It was part of the building's original elaborate water collecting and drainage system. Water from melting snow was collected from the roof by gutters, and then drained down to huge cisterns below the house. In a small room that served as a lavatory, the toilet was a hole in the floor, which was connected to the house's drains.

The rooms on the upper floors were well lit. They were decorated with ornate fireplaces (with decorated plasterwork conical canopies), intricately carved wooden ceilings and latticework (around both internal and external windows), woven carpets, and interesting wooden cupboards. Many of these cupboards were located at the end of a room near to its entrance, and they had galleries above them where women and children were permitted to sit whilst their menfolk discussed matters with guests. These cupboards had two sets of doors. One set opened into the room, and the other into the corridor. Women of the house could deliver, for example, dishes of food or bedding (for guests) into the cupboard from the corridor, and then close the doors so that they remained out of sight of the male guests when the inner doors were opened. The Skenduli family were devout Muslims, practising purdah.

The internal wooden doors had elaborately decorated metal handles, which looked as delicate as fine embroidery. Several decorative motifs pervaded the building. These included the eight- and ten-pointed stars, which were ancient Illyrian symbols. There were plenty of fresh pomegranates as well as a profusion of carved wooden pomegranate flowers (in bas-relief). These signified fertility and prosperity.

Mr Skenduli's tour was magnificent. We felt that we were not looking at a museum but rather at a living home, but we were not because Mr Skenduli has a flat elsewhere in the city. During the Communist period, his house had been used as the town's ethnographic museum. The state had returned it to him, and the contents of the museum had been transferred across the road to the house that is known as Enver Hoxha's birthplace.

At first sight, the current Ethnographic Museum appears to be housed in a home almost as venerable as that of Mr Skenduli. I visited it in 1984, but then we were not told that this was not the actual home of the Hoxha family back in 1908 when Enver was born. The present building stands where the Hoxha family's more modest dwelling *used* to be. Blendi Fevzi explained in his recent book *Enver Hoxha: The Iron Fist of Albania*:

"... the communist chief's family and residence were never regarded as part of the town's prominent clique – a tightly knit clique extremely proud of their roots, traceable back to mediaeval times..."

In contrast, the Kadare family (see below) were part of that 'clique'.

Hoxha's original family home burnt down in the early 1960s. A new grander residence, the present museum building, was built in 1966 in the traditional style of patrician Gjirokastër houses. It was designed by Enver Hoxha's sister. Enver's 'improved' birthplace lacked the charm and genuineness of real old buildings such as the Skenduli and the Kotoni houses. The museum, whose rooms simulate the kind of rooms that we saw in the Skenduli house, contained lovely artefacts, but felt sterile.

A young man in the Ethnographic Museum invited us to see the house in which the author Ismail Kadare, one of my favourite novelists, was born. I followed him down some treacherously steep cobbled alleyways, leaving Lopa to sit in the shade of some trees near the high school. Kadare's former home fell into disrepair, but has recently been almost totally reconstructed; only the lower courses of brickwork were original. The result was very beautiful. Craftsmen have carved wooden ceilings and doors in the traditional style, just as we saw at the Skenduli House. When Kadare visited it recently, he approved of what had been done. Much of the building was being used to exhibit contemporary paintings. There were only a few exhibits relating to the author's life. I saw photographs of Ismail as a child, some of his books, and most interestingly a pith helmet. Kadare wore it when he visited Vietnam in the late 1960s, during the Vietnam War. I found it ironic that the helmet was placed on the flag of the USA, the enemy of the Viet-Cong. There was also a metal 'treasure chest' bearing the date 1889. This belonged to the Kadare family, and had been donated by Ismail's sister.

After clambering up an almost vertical street appropriately named Rruga Sokaku i të Marrëve (Mad Men's Alley) in the blistering heat, Lopa and I went to a café with a shaded terrace overlooking the roofs of the old town. We noticed a monumental concrete scroll towering above a venerable building. This scroll commemorated the first Albanian school (as distinct from Greek schools or Islamic madrasahs) in the city. It was opened in 1886. While we were sipping our coffees, an ambulance stopped outside a house nearby. A white coated man entered the house. Some hours later, when I went for an afternoon stroll, I noticed a wooden coffin painted light blue, resting vertically next to the house's front door.

We walked into the old bazaar area past the city's headquarters of The Democratic Party. This is led by Dr Sali Berisha, a cardiologist, whose 'reigns' as Albania's post-Communist leader have aroused mixed reactions amongst Albanians. We entered a souvenir shop at the point where five steep cobbled roads meet. This sold a large variety of goods. Mugs and 'fridge magnets bearing the faces of Enver Hoxha and Mother Teresa jostled each other with unintended intimacy on crowded shelves. Hoxha would not allow Teresa to visit Albania, but his successor Ramiz Alia permitted her to do so in 1989. Anne Sebba wrote in her book

Mother Teresa that the famous nun laid flowers on Hoxha's gravestone in Tirana. In 'exchange', she was permitted to open two 'houses' where her sisters could work with the poor.

The shop was run by Jonida, who pointed out another souvenir shop opposite hers, which, she told us, had been the only such shop during the Hoxha era. It is now run by her mother. I asked Jonida whether the state-run hotel, where I stayed in 1984, still existed. She told us to go downhill to the square named Sheshi Çerçiz Topulli, where the original hotel, now called 'Hotel Çajupi', stood.

Çerçiz Topulli (1880-1915) was an Albanian patriot, who formed a band of Albanian guerrillas in Sofia (Bulgaria). In 1905, they killed the commander of the Turkish constabulary in Gjirokastër. The hotel that stands on the square was named after Andon Çajupi (1866-1930), a poet and playwright. He was born in Sheper in the Zagori Mountains north-east of Gjirokastër. I stayed in this hotel in 1984. It has been modernised since then, but has kept one room from the Hoxha period, a lounge, in its original state. This was decorated with carved wood panelling and some well-preserved frescoes, which at first sight looked almost pre-Raphaelite. The exquisitely painted scenes, in the socialist-realism style, depicted aspects of modern (i.e. pre-1990) life. Some of the rustic landscapes contained electric pylons and oil derricks. In one domestic scene, there was a modern briefcase in the foreground, and another depicted washing lines with laundry hanging on them. I was glad to see that these skilfully executed works of art have been preserved.

We ate lunch in the spacious restaurant on the hotel's top floor. It had wonderful views of the old bazaar with its tiled grey roofed buildings piled one above another, and beyond them the patrician mansions perched on the mountainside beneath the castle. When we had eaten, the waiter asked us to tell the lady chef how much we had enjoyed her food. Her face lit up when we told her.

A little way downhill from the hotel we spotted the Greek Consulate. This was not present during my visit in 1984, when relations between Greece and Albania were frosty. On a wall, next to the consulate, faded tiles spelled out in huge letters "Lavdi" on one line and "Shqiperise" on another below it. Alone, the two words ('glory' and 'of Albania') made little sense, but it was obvious that they used to be separated by another line of letters, which had been crudely removed. The missing words might have been 'Socialist Party' or something similar. This wall was close to the Town Hall of Gjirokastër. Just outside the Town Hall there was a small kiosk serving as a tourist office. Its staff were sitting outside it, basking in the sun.

We asked to visit the town bunker. A young lady, who spoke good English, took us to a grim little yard behind the Town Hall, and then unlocked an iron gate. We followed her past several heavy rusting thick metal doors into a long underground tunnel lined with wooden doors, each of which led into a small room. We had entered a warren of underground tunnels and chambers that was to have served as a bomb-proof shelter for the government of the city had it ever come under attack by enemy forces.

The construction of the bunker, which was designed to shelter up to two hundred people, began in 1970 and was completed in 1985. It was never used. Gradually, it filled up with water. In 2010, the tunnels were dried out, cleaned, and then opened for public viewing. Although some considerable restoration work was undertaken to make the tunnels safe, many original features were left just as they were found after re-opening the complex. Much of what remains from before its re-opening was rotting mildewed, or rusting, furniture.

Near the entrance, there was a sofa with fading green and yellow checked upholstery stained with splashes of the white paint used to restore the walls of the tunnels. The doors of each of the rooms were labelled as they had been when the place was built. Most of the rooms were offices. For example, there were rooms for top officials, medical personnel, secretaries, 'dactylographers', police officials, political education officers, party secretaries, and so on. In some of them there were abandoned bedstead frames, tables, chests of drawers, chairs, stools, and a typewriter.

One long tunnel led to another, all of them lined with labelled doors. We saw the dining hall, the kitchen, the toilets (there were six cubicles for two hundred people), the meeting hall, and the air-conditioning plant complete with the rusting remnants of an old-fashioned air-conditioning machine. In some of the tunnels, the metal ducts, rectangular in cross-section, for circulating air were still in place. We were shown many rooms and tunnels, but were informed that they were only a small part of the whole underground complex. Visiting this reminded me of a similar, but smaller, subterranean bunker built by the Nazis near Mariahilferstrasse in the centre of Vienna (Austria) in the early 1940s. When I visited the city in 1971, I stayed in one of the rooms in the bunker, which was then being used as a youth hostel. Like the bunker in Gjirokastër, the one in Vienna consisted of long tunnels lined by small rooms. Unlike that in Gjirokastër, the air-conditioning system in the youth hostel still functioned; it had been installed by the Nazis.

After emerging into the sunshine, we had drinks on the terrace of the MAPO Restaurant close to the Hotel Çajupi. Built in 1907, the restaurant premises became, for a while, the local Magazin Popullore (acronym: MAPO: Peoples' Store). A young girl, a Roma, stared at us from behind a large potted plant. Across the road, there was a wall on which there were bas-relief busts of some of the city's literary worthies. These included Ismail Kadare; the expert linguist Eqrem Çabej (1908-1980); and the poet Musine Kokalari (c.1917-1983).

Kokolari, the first recognised female Albanian writer, founded the Albanian Social Democratic Party in 1943. After WW2, she was persecuted by the Communist regime and died poor and isolated. Before her arrest by the Communists, she had a house in Gjirokastër, which has recently (2014) been restored. At her trial in 1946, she said (reported on Pen International's website):

"I don't need to be a communist to love my country. I love my country even though I am not a communist. I love its progress. You boast that you have won the war, and now you are the winner you want to extinguish those who you call political opponents. I think differently from you but I love my country…"

In 1993, the post-Communist government recognised her posthumously as a 'martyr of Democracy'.

After resting at the Kotoni, I took a stroll during which I saw the coffin, mentioned above. Close to the Ethnographic Museum, I entered a small shop. Its shelves were stacked mainly with boxes and cans of imported food, mostly from Italy. The small shop also sold fresh eggs and, what I was seeking, scissors. Before I could pay for them, the shopkeeper insisted on cutting a piece of paper to demonstrate that they were sharp.

Near to Enver Hoxha's 'birth house', I noticed a wall with some roughly painted graffiti that read in, what even I could tell, was incorrect Albanian: "Long live Enver Hoxha". On the wall of his house, the words "16 Tetor 1908, Enveri ljegjendar" (16th October 1908, the legendary Enver) had been crudely sprayed in red paint against a white background. The date was Enver's birthday. Evidently, he is not universally condemned in Albania.

Next, I saw a toy doll nailed above a gateway. All over Albania, we saw weathered dolls and other soft toys like teddy bears attached to the outside of buildings. These toys are examples of *dordolec*, objects to ward off the 'evil-eye'. They often looked quite evil when they became weather-beaten. I looked at buildings built in various eras of Albania's history, and in varying states of disrepair. Far across the valley, beyond the new lower part of the city, a wall of mountains, whose creased surface formed a picturesque horizon, separated the district of Gjirokastër from that of Përmet.

We ate dinner in the old bazaar area in an attractive first-floor restaurant. The Restaurant Odaja had a pleasant interior with a balcony overlooking the street, but the food was unexceptional. The waiter, who might have been the owner, was very grumpy about serving us *uje cesme* (tap water), which attracts no charge.

Mr Skenduli pointing to a typical conical Ottoman fireplace in Gjirokastër.

Fresco in the bar of the Hotel Çajupi in Gjirokastër.
Note the depiction of the city's old houses in the background.

Mugshots:
Enver Hoxha and Mother ('Nene') Tereza in a souvenir shop in Gjirokastër.

Saranda, Butrint, Shën Vasil, Porto Palermo, Himara

Friday, 3rd of June 2016 The direction signs along the good road between Gjirokastër to Saranda were bilingual: Albanian and Greek. This is because many Greek speaking Albanians live in this area. In 1984, when travelling in this district, I visited one of the Greek minority villages. It looked just like any other Albanian village, except that the propaganda notices extolling Enver Hoxha's regime were in Greek rather than in Albanian (see illustration below). Also, on that trip, we passed an Orthodox church, the thirteenth century St Nicholas, stranded on a rise, like a small island, surrounded by fields at Mesopotam near Saranda. This time, we tried to reach the church. We followed a farm track towards it only to find that it was surrounded by a high fence with locked gates.

Socialist slogans in a 'Greek' village near Gjirokastër in 1984

When I compared my photograph of the Bay of Saranda in 1984 with that taken in 2016, it was difficult to believe that it was taken in the same place. What had been a small, sleepy seaside resort in the south of Albania has become a concrete jungle. Almost every available space within a few hundred metres of the sea shore has been occupied by new buildings. Driving through this overbuilt area was depressing. Yet, Saranda has become very popular with Albanian and Kosovar holiday makers.

The urban sprawl developing around Saranda is currently limited at the south of the city by the Butrint National Park. However, the village of Ksamil is beginning to expand within this green area. From Ksamil, houses on Corfu were clearly visible across the short stretch of water that separates it from Albania. We drove through Ksamil, and reached the archaeological park that contains some of the ruins of what was once the large ancient city of Butrint (Buthrotum in Latin). Its origins date back to before the first millennium BC. As the ruins are well described in guidebooks, I shall not try to compete.

Albania was visited in the early nineteenth century by Lord Byron and his companion John Hobhouse, who noted in his *A Journey through Albania, and other provinces of Turkey in Europe and Asia, to Constantinople, during the years 1809 and 1810* that:

"Butrinto (near which, if we may credit Pouqueville, are to be seen some remains of the lofty city of "Buthrotum") was so long in the possession of the Venetians…"

The French diplomat Francois Pouqueville (1770-1838) visited Butrint in early 1806 and saw ruins of the ancient city. He wrote:

"To judge by the present vestiges the town was built around an eminence crowned by the acropolis or castle ... The ruins ...are an aqueduct, supported on brick arcades with buttresses. Among the ruins of houses are some probably public buildings, surrounded by columns not circular, but cut into eight faces. ... Among the ruins are also found Gothic capitals ... evidence of the fixed abode of the nations from the north of Europe..."

The Frenchman's description seems remarkably accurate, so I believe that we may credit him with having seen the ancient remains. From what Hobhouse wrote, it is unlikely that he and Byron visited the ruins of ancient Butrint. This conflicts with what I have read in some guidebooks and, also, in the excellently laid out museum in the archaeological site. The two Englishmen might have visited the district of Butrint, but maybe not the ruins, which were not properly excavated until the 1920s. Another Englishman, Edward Lear, visited Butrint in the late 1840s. He made sketches of its walls from Ksamil. Much earlier, Aeneas is reported to have passed through Butrint on his way from Troy to Italy. So, wrote Virgil a few years before Christ's birth.

The ruins of Butrint were located amongst shady trees, which made walking around them pleasurable. Occasionally, we caught glimpses of the sea or the Vivari Channel, which connects the Lake of Butrint to the Ionian Sea. From the acropolis, where a well laid-out museum is located, there are magnificent views towards the mountains on the Greek border, the Vivari Channel, and the triangular fortress (built by Ali Pasha) that lies across it. We saw fishermen at work on the lake and mussel cultivation beds, which I remember seeing in 1984.

The ruins of Butrint reflect the early history of Albania. It was settled by the Illyrians, the Hellenes, and the Romans. George Ostrogorsky, in his *History of the Byzantine State*, wrote that Butrint and other towns in southern Albania were constantly being captured and then lost by rival armies during the Middle Ages. The Albturist *Tourist Guidebook Guide of Albania* (1969), says that Butrint was also:

"... captured by the Normans (XIth century), by Manfred of the Hohenstaufens (XIIIth century) and by the Venetians (XIVth century). At the end of the XVIIIth century the French also came to the fortress of

Butrint but were chased away by the powerful ruler of Albania of that time - Ali Pasha Tepelena. This Albanian feudal lord fortified the place with two small fortresses - one at the entrance of the canal and the other opposite the ancient town."

During the Italian occupation of Albania, Mussolini's son-in-law Count Ciano is said to have preferred Butrint to other places in the country because of its pleasant surroundings. On the 25th of May 1940, he noted in his diary:

"Stopped at Butrinto. Very beautiful."

Little has changed in this respect.

When Enver Hoxha brought Khrushchev to Butrint in May 1959, he was horrified by the Russian's reaction to it. In his memoirs, *The Kruschchevites*, Hoxha wrote:

"However, Khrushchev was truly an ignoramus in these fields. He could see only the 'profitability': "Why are these things of value to you? Do they increase the well-being of the people?" he asked me. He called Malinovsky, at that time minister of defence, who was always at hand. "Look, how marvellous this is!", I heard them whisper. "An ideal base for our submarines could be built here. These old things should be dug up and thrown into the sea (they were referring to the archaeological finds at Butrint). We can tunnel through this mountain to the other side", and he pointed to Ksamil. "We shall have the most ideal and most secure base in the Mediterranean. From here we can paralyze and attack everything."

Hoxha who, despite his disastrous actions, was a cultured man added:

"It made my flesh creep to hear them talk like this, as if they were the masters of the seas, countries and peoples. "No, Nikita Khrushchev", I said to myself, "we shall never allow you to set out to enslave other countries and shed their peoples' blood from our territory. You will never have Butrint, Vlora, or any inch of the Albanian territory, to use for those evil purposes.""

We enjoyed viewing Ancient Greek and Roman remains, the beautiful ruins of an early circular (Christian) baptistery and the basilica nearby, and an Ottoman fortress tower. We walked around the old city walls until we reached the Lion Gate. A bas-relief carving on its headstone looked like a bull or buffalo, but experts say it is a lion gnawing at the head of a bull with horns.

After two and a half hours of exploration, we returned to our car, and then drove it onto the basic ferry that crosses the Vivari Channel. As it did in 1984, it consisted of a small rectangular raft covered with irregularly laid wooden planks. The raft, which has no engine, is dragged silently across the water by cables attached to a motor housed on the southern bank. Since 1990, this venerable craft has carried many more vehicles per day than it did in 1984, reflecting Albania's post-Communist boom in motor vehicle usage.

The small section of southern Albania between Butrint and Greece contains the town of Konispol, which is very close to the Greek border. This town became a home to Muslim Cham (*Çamë*) Albanians. They have had a sad recent history. Until the end of WW2, these people, fiercely nationalistic Albanians, lived in what is now north-western Greece. At the end of WW2, the Greeks, who accused them of collaborating with the fascist armies, expelled them, and chased them into Albania.

During the Greek Civil War that followed WW2, many Greek children were abducted by the Communists from villages in north-west Greece close to Albania, and were re-settled in parts of Communist Eastern Europe, where they grew up. Many of them passed through Albania where they were cared for by the partisans and their widows. *Eleni*, written by Nicolas Gage, told the story of a mother, who was killed protecting her children from abduction. Eleni and her family lived in Lia, which is in Greece about eighteen mountainous kilometres northeast of Konispol and only three kilometres from Albania.

After disembarking from the ferry, we drove past Ali Pasha's triangular Ottoman fortress and through the village of Xarrë, where a young man stopped us at a T-junction. In good English, he asked us where we were heading. We told him Saranda. He said that we were going in the wrong direction. In a way, he was right because the main road went via Ksamil, but we wanted to try another route that avoided both Ksamil and the centre of Saranda. We told him that we were going to Pllakë, which was on our route. We were astonished when he leapt into our car, and sat on the back seat. He told us that he had been waiting for a *furgon* (a privately-owned passenger carrying minivan that plies between settlements in Albania) going to Saranda and needed a lift. The word *furgon* derives from the French *fourgon*, meaning 'van'. The British novelist Georgette Heyer refers to these conveyances frequently in her novels set in Regency England (the first two decades of the nineteenth century). Albanian *furgons* travel, like the so-called 'black taxis' in South Africa, from A to B, stopping wherever a passenger wishes to embark or disembark.

Our uninvited backseat 'guest' told us that he had worked in Athens as a house-painter, but had returned to Albania when the economy collapsed in Greece. He was one of the multitude of Albanians, who left home to work across the border. As we drove along, he pointed out various features in the countryside, which I cannot recall because I was concerned that it was going to be difficult to persuade him to leave us. I need not have worried because he asked to be dropped off at a busy road junction outside Saranda, where *furgons* passed frequently.

Avoiding the centre of Saranda, we headed northwest along an inland road, and, after crossing a mountain pass, we reached the village of Shën Vasil. When Oakley-Hill visited it in the 1930s, he remembered that:

"The soft shadiness of Shën Vasil came as came as a relief to the eye and mind."

Little has altered. We parked in the village's circular 'piazza', in the middle of which there was a large old tree well-endowed with leafy branches. It was surrounded by a low, white painted circular wall, on which two elderly gentlemen were seated next to each other, enjoying the shade. They remained there the whole time we were in the village, and watched me as I dashed around taking photographs.

A well-maintained Communist WW2 memorial listed seventeen 'martyrs' who fell in the National War of Liberation. Of these, four came from one family and four from another. Roderick Bailey wrote in his book about the SOE that in June 1944 the partisans in Shën Vasil and in nearby Himara fought the Germans, who were attacking them and their SOE allies. There was another monument, painted in dark green, bearing the date 29th of November, 1969. Somewhat damaged, this was surmounted by the Communist star under which the word "Lavdi" (glory) could be discerned. The best-preserved part of the monument was a bas-relief of a short lady with a basket over her left arm. Her right arm was raised while she appeared to be picking something from above, maybe grapes. There were grapevines growing close to the memorial. The 29th of

November 1969 was the twenty-fifth anniversary of the liberation of Albania by the Communist forces.

Several cafés surrounded the circular open space. Only the grandiose, rather glitzy, 'Studio Max Bar Restaurant' served food. It advertised in English that it was an "Exchange Bikers Stop", where Greek, English, Spanish, and Italian was spoken. The reference to bikers, none of whom stopped here during our short stay in Shën Vasil, is significant. We saw many leather-clad motorcyclists from all over Europe travelling in Albania on powerful 'bikes.

We ate a delicious lunch of fresh salad and cheeses with slices of fresh bread grilled on only one side (a common accompaniment in Albania). We were also served *salce kosi* flavoured with olive oil and fresh oregano. The owner, an Albanian Greek, spoke many languages because he had worked as a sailor on cruise liners for fifteen years. He told us that all the food he served was grown by him, and was free of what he called "metasulphates". The cheeses were made from his sister's goats' milk. While we sat on the restaurant's raised terrace, hardly any traffic passed apart from a few heavily laden donkeys with their owners walking alongside them or sitting side-saddle, which is how Albanians ride on the wooden saddles that they commonly use. At one stage, a car with the marking "Antikontrabanda" pulled up next to our parked car, examined it cursorily, and then sped off.

A faded old road sign in Shën Vasil, which looked as if it might have predated the Communist period, indicated that we were still twenty-two kilometres from our destination. We continued our journey along a winding main road that passed through spectacular mountainous scenery. We were near the sea, but separated from it by a mountainous ridge. After passing through Borsh, which was close to the inlet that was used by the British SOE as a makeshift port during WW2, the road broke through the hills and began running along the coast in a northerly direction. Near Borsh, we skirted around a cow relaxing in the middle of the main road just like cows do in India. For most of the way, the road ran high above the sea, but occasionally it curled down to reach sea-level to cross the estuaries of the numerous creeks, which flow down from the wall of mountains that isolates this coastal part of southern Albania from the rest of the country. Around every corner, there were wonderful views, each one different from the others.

We had entered what used to be called 'Chimarra' or 'Xhimarra'. According to Pouqueville (writing in 1820 about his visit to Albania in 1805):

"... in the present time, no part of the coast of Epirus possesses air of greater purity and salubrity than the western slopes of the mountains of Chimara. But the advantages of health and long life enjoyed by the Chimariotes are more than compensated by the nature and appearance of the country allotted to them. Naked mountains intersected by tremendous gulfs and inaccessible precipices announce a region of incurable sterility. But these precipices and gulfs and rocks are regarded by the natives as their main defence against all enemies. Hence the insuperable attachment of the Chimariotes to his native deserts..."

Hobhouse, writing in 1813, paints a different picture of this district:

"The soil in the valleys of Chimera yield olives and maize in great quantities, but not many vines. The inhabitants contrive to lay as much of the produce of their lands, as, with the fleeces of their flocks, and the gall-nuts and timber of their forests, enables them to supply themselves with arms, and carry on a small traffic at Valona, and Porto Palermo, and in the small ports on their coast."

More than one hundred and twenty years later, Oakley-Hill noted that in this district olive tree covered hills sloped down to the sea and:

"Much citrus fruit was grown there too and a special kind, sought by Jews, was exported to Palestine."

Probably, he was referring to the *etrog - Citrus medica*, used by Jewish people during the week-long holiday of Succoth. The importance of Albanian *etrogs* (*etrogim*) is highlighted in an article in the *Jerusalem Post* of 16th October 2005 that describes how in 1846:

"Alexander Ziskind Mintz, a learned resident of Brody who earned his livelihood from selling etrogim ... published a booklet titled *Pri Etz Hadar* that prohibited the etrogim of Corfu and the surrounding areas such as the Albanian coast. It seems that a former partner of his had broken off and set up shop in these new areas."

In 1935, the British Zionist journalist Leo Elton visited Albania with a view to it becoming a new homeland for the Jews. During his visit, he remarked that the oranges and lemons grown there were amongst the best in the world, and the Jews' success in raising oranges in pre-state Israel could be replicated in Albania. Elton liked the Albanians, but the project never took-off, partly because the country did not have enough concert halls and theatres!

Elton's instincts about the Albanians proved accurate. During WW2, Albanians risked their lives to protect Jewish refugees from being captured by the Germans. They were so successful that after WW2 there were more Jews in Albania than before. This was the only axis-occupied country where the number of Jews increased between 1939 and 1945.

This coastal stretch of southern Albania, which runs from the Llogara Pass (see below) south-east to Borsh, is now part of the 'Albanian Riviera'. Being separated from the rest of the country by high mountains and bounded by the sea, this part of Albania took longer to be conquered by the Ottomans, and because of its maritime contacts with Italy maintained a way of life different from the rest of the country. Although visited by Byron and then later by Edward Lear, this isolated coastal strip used to be one of the least-known places in Europe. Now, with its lovely beaches it has become one of the most frequently visited parts of Albania.

On the southern side of the Bay of Porto Palermo, we saw a small peninsula. It was connected to the mainland by a thin causeway. Atop this rocky projection of land, sat the Castle of Ali Pasha silhouetted against the bright sun that was now low in the sky. It might have been built long before Ali arrived, possibly by the Venetians. Pouqueville remarked:

"It consists of a square with bastions, having a few guns, of no service either to command the entrance or to protect the shipping at anchor."

North of the fortress across the Bay of Porto Palermo we spotted the southern entrance to the Porto Palermo Tunnel, a Communist era creation. Constructed in Enver Hoxha's time, a short canal leads from the bay to the concrete ringed entrance of a tunnel that runs beneath a headland. This tunnel, circular in cross-section, was built to hide naval craft including submarines. Near the tunnel, whose entrance looked well-maintained, there was a compound containing several low buildings, most of which seemed abandoned. There were a few vehicles parked amongst them, and an Albanian flag was fluttering from a flag post next to a white painted shelter, rather like a small bus-shelter, inside of which an Albanian flag had been painted.

After crossing a forested headland, we descended into the beautiful Bay of Himara, where we were to spend a couple of nights in the well-appointed Rondos Hotel. Our room had a balcony which overlooked an idyllic bay surrounded by verdant hills. We had a view across the sea to the northern Ionian Greek islands of Eriekoussa, Platia, and the more distant Corfu. Conical straw umbrellas were in abundance all along the clean sandy beach, but there were few people about. On the horizon, a large ferry boat moved slowly towards Greece.

When the Ottomans invaded the Balkans in the fifteenth century, many people from the district that includes modern day Himara fled to Italy, where their descendants live to this day. We visited the town of Piana degli Albanesi in western Sicily in 2014. Almost all of its seven thousand inhabitants are descendants of Albanians who left the Balkans in the late fifteenth century. Although they are all fluent in Italian, their mother tongue is an archaic form of southern Albanian (ie. Tosk) called Arbëresh. Some of the original settlers in Piana, which was founded by Albanian refugees in 1488, came from Himara. We were not staying in the old part of the town high above the bay where they once lived, but beneath it close to the beach from which they might have set sail.

Hobhouse, who visited the area in 1810 with Lord Byron wrote of Himara (which he called 'Chimera'):

"Chimera once had a fortress defended by 300 Turks ... The Chimeriotes near the sea are many of them Christians, but in the interior they are nearly all Turks. They are barbarous and warlike; and though all of them are at peace with, or perhaps almost under the subjection of Ali, their different villages are in a state of perpetual warfare against each other..."

After watching the sun set over the Adriatic and the beach umbrellas had been folded up for the night, we walked along the seafront to the Taverna Stoli. We had a table on the terrace overlooking the dark water in the bay. When we arrived, there was an Orthodox priest with a long white beard sitting nearby. Wearing a flat-topped conical black *kalimavkion* on his head, he looked just like priests in Greece. A long table near ours was laid out for a banquet. Several bottles of expensive Italian mineral water were placed amongst the wine glasses and other tableware. We ate delicious, fresh seafood, including superb grilled squid. It was served by Maria, who was very friendly, an Albanian whose mother tongue is Greek like that of many others who lived in the district. When we asked Maria in English whether she would be on duty the next evening, she very sweetly patted her chest and said: "I am".

Before retiring to bed, we telephoned Driton, who lived in Vlorë, one of Albania's main sea ports, and arranged to meet him the next day.

Monastery of St Nicholas at Mesopotam, near Saranda.

Ferry across the Vivara Channel at Butrint. Ali Pasha's castle in the background.

Porto Palermo. The arrow points to the 'Cold War' era tunnel's entrance.

Llogara, Vlorë, Old Himara

Saturday, 4th June 2016 After eating a sumptuous breakfast, which included much fresh fruit, at the Rondos Hotel, we set off for Vlorë along the coastal road. We stopped to refuel with diesel near Vuno at a Kastrati filling station. There, we watched two young men having litre plastic mineral water bottles filled with petrol. Both had lighted cigarettes in their hands.

After passing through several coastal towns that clung onto the steep mountain slopes which rise straight from the sea, we reached the southern base of the Llogara Pass. In 1964, Albert Mahuzier crossed this pass with his wife in his Renault 4L on a road that must have been monstrous. He wrote (in French, kindly translated by Prof. E Langille) the following after crossing the pass:

"But the joys of having conquered the Llogara made up for these new worries and at 3 o'clock with a full stomach, and the Renault 4 spitting up black juice and noxious black smoke, we definitively turned our backs on the vertiginous meanders of the downward slope."

More than 100 years before Mahuzier crossed this pass, Edward Lear made the same journey (in 1848). Like Mahuzier, he was travelling south, towards Himara (Khimara). After reaching the summit, Lear wrote:

"… we began to descend, and soon emerged from the clouds into bright sunlight, which lit up all the difficulties of what is called the Strada Bianca, or Aspri Ruga - a zig-zag path on the side of the steepest of precipices, yet the only communication between Khimara and Avlona [i.e Vlorë] towards the north. The track is a perfect staircase, and were you to attempt to ride down it, you would seem at each angle as if about to shoot off into the blue sea below you; even when walking down, one comes to an intimate knowledge of what a fly must feel in traversing a ceiling or perpendicular wall."

Since Lear and the French couple made their intrepid journeys, the pass has been improved. We ascended the wild southern slopes (with few trees) by way of a well-engineered series of inclines linked by tightly curved hairpin bends, and reached the top of the pass, 1043 metres above sea level.

The descent northwards towards Vlorë was more difficult than the ascent from the south: the road was steeper and narrower, and the curves much tighter. We had time to enjoy the forested scenery of the northern slopes because we were stuck behind a slow-moving bus on a road where overtaking would have been suicidal. Halfway down the slopes of Mount Çika, part of which we were crossing, we saw a large mosaic made during the Hoxha years. Its fading tiles depicted partisans in various poses, some with firearms. Its text commemorated fighting that occurred in this district. It was dedicated to the victory of the partisans from nearby Dukat over the Germans, on the 11th of September, 1943. When Edward Lear passed through Dukat in 1848, he was plagued by fierce dogs in that village.

We reached the coastal plain near Orikum (close to the site of the Ancient Greek town of Ὤρικος), and began speeding towards Vlorë. We approached the city along its corniche or *'lungomare'* (as some Albanians call it). I had not originally included Vlorë on our itinerary because I had feared wrongly that it would be over-modernised, but I was pleased that Driton invited us.

On the landward side of the *lungomare* we noticed many new buildings and much building work. The result was more tasteful than what we had seen in Saranda. At the end of this road, we drove along a wide boulevard that led from the port to the city centre. With wide pavements, this grand street was lined with buildings that were built before, during, and after, the Communist period. Those built before WW2 were particularly elegant. The boulevard was named after Sadik Zotaj (1921-1943), a local boy who was killed by the Nazis in WW2. We stopped near the sixteenth century Murat Mosque (built by the great Ottoman architect Mimar Sinan [1489-1588]), and met Driton. According to the writer Philip Ward in his 1983 guide to Albania, the Communists were then using the mosque as an artists' studio.

Driton greeted us like old friends, even though it was our first meeting. We got on well from the beginning. Speaking good English and even better Italian, he helped us appreciate his city. Very close to the mosque, we saw the well-maintained residence of Ismail Qemal Vlora (1844-1919), the founder of independent Albania and its first head of state. Outside this building and opposite the mosque, we saw a memorial to Artur Rustemi. He was killed during riots that erupted following the failure of the pyramid investment schemes in 1997. Aged thirty-three, he was shot by the police on the 10th of February 1997. A report in the *Irish Times* published two days later noted:

"… around 30,000 people turned out for his funeral yesterday, clapping as his coffin was hoisted out of the crumbling apartment block where he had lived and into the street … Minutes later, flames engulfed the nearby headquarters of President Sali Berisha's ruling right-wing Democratic Party. It was not immediately clear what had caused the fire. Seeing the black smoke belching from the whitewashed building, a huge cheer went up and Mr Rustemi's open coffin was carried high alongside the blaze. 'Berisha you clown, don't mess with our town,' the crowd chanted as it inched forward down the main palm-lined boulevard, three men carrying Albanian flags leading the way."

Many Albanians believe that Berisha was in part responsible for the trouble and financial ruin that the pyramid schemes caused them.

We walked to the Independence Monument in Independence Square. A bold ensemble of men surrounding a flag-bearer was sculpted in the socialist-realism style. One of its team of sculptors was the Communist politician Kristaq Rama (1932-1988), father of the present Prime Minister Edi Rama. This lofty monument was set in a rectangular grassy open space. Nearby, we saw the grave of Ismail Qemal Vlora, who died suddenly (of a stroke or heart condition) in Perugia (Italy). Driton told us that Qemal's final words to his children were:

"I have nothing to leave you but the future of Albania."

There was another memorial to Albania's independence, a flag-pole mounted on a tall stone plinth that bears the date "28 XI 1912", the date that Albania became independent, and some double-headed eagles, all in stark bas-relief. On a hill above the square and visible from it, we could see a cemetery for the martyrs who died during WW2 with a gigantic Communist-style war memorial alongside its entrance.

We had coffee with Driton in the sun-drenched garden of a modern café close to a warren of narrow streets lined by picturesque old buildings with Italianate wooden shutters. He discussed the attempts of recent Greek Governments to Hellenise Albanians. I had seen a fading political poster in Greek in a window in a village between Gjirokastër and Mesopotam. It encouraged electors to vote for the Greek political party, MEGA-EMMM ('Greek Minority Party for the Future', allied with Sali Berisha's Democratic Party). This party promoted Greek Nationalism in Albania. Driton said that many (Greek minority) Albanians have accepted Greek passports, but few of them vote for the Greek political parties in Albania. In addition, most of the Albanian Greek speakers living in southern Albania around Gjirokastër in villages (such as in Dropulli district) sing songs in Albanian. When someone is born, or dies, celebrations and dirges are sung in Albanian rather than Greek.

Driton had worked in Greece. When he arrived there, the first thing he was asked was his religion. He had replied that if there is a God, it did not matter how you worship him. If more people thought like Driton, there would be less trouble in the world. He said that in general the Albanians in Greece worked much harder than the local Greeks. In fact, they work so hard that some Albanian migrants in Greece have been successful enough to employ Greeks in Greece.

After coffee, we returned to our car with Driton. Before we boarded, he pointed out a statue that depicted an important Bektashi 'Baba' (priest). The Bektashis are a sect, a dervish order, of Muslims that have merged concepts from Sufism with some from Shia Islam. Adherents of Bektashism, a popular 'branch' or 'version' of Islam in Albania, drink alcohol and are liberal in material matters compared with other Muslims. They also share some features of other religions, such as Buddhism and Zoroastrianism. They believe that hidden inner beliefs are far more important than external manifestations of faith. The statue stood at the foot of the flight of stairs leading up a hill to the supposed final resting place of the Bektashi spiritual leader Kuzum Baba (aka: Sejjid Ali Sulltan).

We drove Driton 'downtown' (as he put it) to the port area, where we visited the small two-storey building from which Ismail Qemal Vlora proclaimed the independence of Albania. Formerly a Turkish quarantine hospital (or dispensary), this house became the first home of the government of independent Albania. Now, it houses the Museum of Independence. In the 2001 edition of Pettifer's *Blue Guide to Albania*, what has become the museum was described as:

"…a small 19 C house that is now a café. On the wall is a plaque noting it is where Ismail Qemal proclaimed the independence of…"

The building was neither mentioned in Pettifer's 1994 guide, nor in Philip Ward's 1983 book. However, it is mentioned in the 1969 Albturist guide:

"The Museum of Independence is housed in a historic building, associated with the Proclamation of the Independence of Albania. The materials exhibited here illustrate the struggle of the people for freedom and independence…"

This small building of great historic importance was dwarfed by huge cranes and ocean-going freighters in the nearby port area. Its windows had slatted wooden shutters, and there was a balcony projecting over its main entrance. It was from this balcony that Ismail Qemal read the declaration of Albania's independence in 1912. Vlorë, which was invaded by the Italians in 1914, was the country's first capital. In 1920, Tirana assumed this role.

We were guided around the museum, and shown photos, documents, and furniture, connected with the historic events that occurred around 1912. Driton kindly translated our lady guide's interesting commentary into English. Sadly, we were not permitted to stand on the historic balcony because it has become too fragile. As we moved from room to room, I noticed that our guide was becoming more and more interested in Lopa, touching her occasionally. At the end of the tour, she told us that she loves watching the Bollywood films and soap-operas broadcast on Albanian television. It was a pity, she said, that Lopa had not been dressed in a sari. Lopa's arrival in the museum had meant a great deal to her. It was as if one of the characters in the films, which she enjoyed watching, had stepped out of her television and into her museum. She said that Lopa was the first female Indian visitor to the museum since she began working there eleven years earlier.

Near the museum, Driton showed us a large building built in the Communist era. It is now the Rectorate of the University of Vlorë. Previously, this elegant modern building had been the city's Communist Party headquarters. Because of its fine appearance, it had been decided to preserve and restore it. Other buildings have been suffering a different fate. Even some unfinished buildings, such as a hideous skeleton of a skyscraper close to the museum and another by Independence Square, were due to be demolished because they had been determined to be eyesores. Apparently, Prime Minister Edi Rama, who beautified Tirana when he served as its Mayor, has as one of his aims the beautification of Albania. It is said that he roams around the country selecting ugly buildings that need to disappear. This accorded with what we had already learnt about Rama's beautification programme at Lake Ohri.

We stood next to some construction works on the seashore whilst Driton described the three-and-a-half kilometre corniche road being built along the city's seafront. When it is completed, it will become a beautifully landscaped marine drive. We drove back towards the centre of town, stopping at an establishment that I had not expected to find in Albania.

An Israeli patisserie, Pastiçeri Kafe izraelite, has become one of Vlorë's most popular cafés. Its Jewish owner came from Israel. She and her

Israeli husband trained as marine biologists. When he came to Albania and became involved in fish farming, she learnt Albanian in Vlorë, and baking from her mother-in-law. Then, she opened her delightful café. The cakes and pastries that she sells are second to none. People all over Vlorë order cakes for special occasions from her. I ate a portion of perfect apple strudel.

We drove Driton back to where he had left his bicycle. Before meeting him, Lopa and I had thought that we would have be having a quick coffee with him, and then letting him get on with his day. Instead, we spent four highly enjoyable hours with him, and were very pleased that we had been able to do so.

We drove back towards Himara. At the summit of the Llogara Pass, there was a guesthouse and near it a monument bearing a double-headed eagle, a social-realism bas-relief, and the date 1920 (when the first motor road across the pass was built). Then, following in the footsteps of Lear and Mahuzier, we began descending. Halfway down the series of zig-zags, we stopped at an isolated, disused, graffiti-covered cuboid building on a promontory. It commanded a good view of the southern stretch of coast almost as far as the promontory north of Porto Palermo as well as the northern Ionian Greek islands including the coast of distant Corfu. The building's windows were missing and one could easily see into the rooms, whose walls were covered with graffiti. This abandoned edifice had been a Communist-period look-out station where movements of ships, be they Albanian or foreign, could be observed. From these lofty heights, the security forces would have been able to spot vessels containing brave souls trying to flee from Hoxha's Albania, before sending powerful speed boats to intercept them.

Shortly before descending to the beach of Himara, we drove along a side-road to see the remains of old Himara. These were perched on a hill above the sea beneath the ruins of a castle mentioned by Hobhouse (see above). We parked near to a Greek (language) school, housed in a well-restored old building with a plaque in Greek dated 1870. Steep narrow alleyways with grass growing between their cobblestones led up between the mostly abandoned houses of the old town towards the walls of the castle. People from Himara had helped found the town of Piana degli Albanesi in Sicily (in 1488). Maybe, that made me feel that old Himara resembled the Sicilian town. A tourist information sign mentioned that the people of Himara, Orthodox Christians under the leadership of the

Patriarchate of Ohrid, had fought alongside Skanderbeg in his struggles against the Ottoman Turks. When Edward Lear visited old Himara in October 1848, he found it much as we did:

"... Khimara itself - perched on a high isolated rock, the torrent running below it to the sea, with Corfu forming the background to the picture. Khimara is now a ruined place, since its capture by the overwhelming Ali Pasha, but it retains its qualities of convenient asylum for doubtful or fugitive characters..."

In Lear's day, the town was extremely difficult to approach from other parts of Albania, and therefore a suitable refuge for those evading the law.

After watching a fantastic sunset, we returned to the Taverna Stolis. Although we did not order a pizza, I observed that above the restaurant's wood-fired pizza oven there was a crucifix amongst some Greek letters: "IC XC NIKA". The first four letters form a Greek Orthodox 'christogram' (an abbreviation for 'Jesus Christ' in Greek), and 'Nika' means 'conquers'. Talking of Greek, I noticed that the fire extinguisher cabinets in the Hotel Rondos were labelled in both English and Greek, but not in Albanian. Bearing the logo "MBK", these cabinets were made by Mobiak SA, a firm based in Greece. I spotted several products of this company in various buildings we visited all over Albania.

A corner in old Vlorë.

Israeli patisserie in Vlorë

Greek language school in the old part of Himara.

Vlorë, Fier, Apollonia, Ardenicë, Berat

Sunday, 5th June 2016 After crossing the Llogara Pass once more, we stopped in Vlorë at the Pastiçeri Kafe izraelite, and met its owner. Once again, we sampled her baking. She has a light touch, and produces delicate, well-flavoured, delicious patisserie. When we praised her skill, she retorted modestly that anyone could do it, it was just like chemistry: just follow the recipe.

We left Vlorë, somehow missing the beginning of the new highway that was marked on our map. Instead, we found ourselves on a very bumpy road that ran tantalisingly close to the new one along which vehicles were speeding. After missing various unmarked turnings that might have allowed us to join the new motorway, we managed to join it near Novoselë, which is close to the mouth of the River Vjosa.

The city of Fier had grown since 1984. Now larger in extent, it has many tall new buildings. After a series of wrong turns that took us through various backstreets, we joined the Rruga e Semanit that led from the centre towards the sea. Whilst finding our way through Fier, we asked for directions from some dark-skinned people, who looked like Roma. They answered in Greek, as did another passer-by. Greek speakers in Fier included some of the Cham refugees from northern Greece, who settled in Fier and nearby. Robert Elsie, an expert on Albanian matters, wrote in one of his websites (www.albanianphotography.net):

"The Chams were nonetheless given refugee status and allowed to remain in Albania. It was the United Nations Relief and Rehabilitation Administration (UNRRA), active as a relief agency in Albania from September 1945 to the spring of 1947, that provided emergency assistance to the Chams by distributing tents, food and medicine to their squalid camps in Vlora, Fier, ..."

A few kilometres west of Fier, we turned onto a small country lane that led to the archaeological site of Apollonia, which is next to the village of Pojan. We explored the hilly site that contained the ruins of what Hobhouse described as: "... the celebrated city of Apollonia". There would not have been much to see in his time, because there was little that Edward Lear could find there when he visited about thirty years later. He wrote in 1851:

"Taking a peasant from the convent as a guide, I went at sunrise to the single Doric column – the only remaining token of Apollonia above ground. It stands on a dreary little hill, covered with long grass and brambly thorn, and a more lonely and forlorn record of old times cannot well be contemplated."

This city, which thrived in ancient times, was located on the right bank of River Vjosa near its estuary. Now, the meandering river runs south of it. Having already seen the magnificent ruins at Butrint, the remains of Apollonia were an anti-climax. The view from the hillside on which they stand was interesting. Looking away from the sea across a cultivated valley, I spotted four rectangular concrete entrances to what must be an underground bunker (or several bunkers). Each of these looked like openings to staircases or shoots that led downwards. Julian Pettifer wrote that these were entrances to an underground nuclear shelter constructed in 1970.

We ate lunch at a pleasant restaurant on the archaeological site. The food was good, but the service was erratic because the waiters were busy serving a long table at which the earnest looking, rather dour, members of a German tour group were eating. The group looked miserable. After lunch, we drove through Fier, narrowly avoiding a collision with a couple of Mercedes that were chasing each other at great speed and swept past us extremely closely, one on our left and the other on our right.

In 1984, I saw very few cars on the road. Those that I saw were all owned by the state and had been imported. Most of them were either Peugeot saloons or the brick-like Volvo 240 estate cars. A very few of them were Mercedes Benz, which were reserved for the most senior party members only. Today in Albania, the dominant make of car on her roads is Mercedes. Some of them, like those which swept past us in Fier, are the latest models, sleek, aerodynamic, and sporty. They hug the road closely, and are probably quite unsuitable for the ruggedness of most of Albania's road system. They would be good in Tirana or Vlorë, but not in Voskopojë, for example.

The older models of Mercedes are ideal for Albania's roads: they are rugged, robust, and their high wheel-bases allow them to negotiate rocks and other highway obstacles without much risk of damage. Wherever we went, we saw Mercedes of all vintages, many of them looking well-used, often somewhat battered. The older models, of which we saw plenty, have the advantage of being easier to repair than the newer ones that rely over-extensively on sophisticated electronics.

Now, Mercedes are not cheap when bought new. I suspect that many of them that we saw in Albania were second-hand – models that owners elsewhere in Europe had traded in for newer versions. Many of them might have been purchased by family members who had gone abroad to work. I write this to balance what Robin Hanbury-Tenison wrote in *Land of Eagles* (2009):

"Albania is reputed to have the highest Mercedes ownership in the world, almost all stolen from Germany…"

To refute this, let me quote from an article, *In Poor Albania, Mercedes Rules Road*, published in the 10th of November 2002 edition of the reputable *New York Times*:

"Most of the used vehicles on sale here have been imported perfectly legally. Many still bear the temporary registration plates that allow cars to be driven out of Germany and sold abroad, most often in Eastern Europe."

In fairness, maybe many stolen cars landed up in Albania in the 1990s, but by 2002, as the quote suggests, this was no longer the case. Sadly, outside Albania and even amongst some of my more intelligent friends the association of the country with car theft persists. It is true that the Mercedes might be regarded as a high-end luxury car, but that only applies to brand new models. Mercedes that have been around for several years become affordable purchases, even for people living in such a poor country as Albania.

At Kolonjë north of Fier, we left the main road to reach Ardenicë. A winding lane led up a hill to a walled monastery. It was established in the thirteenth century, and was the site of Skanderbeg's marriage to Andronika ('Donika') Arianiti in 1451. We parked near a man selling a poor selection of snacks and drinks, and then climbed the gravel path leading to the monastery's locked outer wooden doors. There was a mentally disturbed beggar hovering beside the path and an old man, also a beggar, sitting a little further up. No one else was about.

We banged hard on the locked door, using its heavy cast-iron knocker. The door was opened by a caretaker, who showed us some of what was within the triangular compound. He pointed to the monks' quarters and some workshops, neither of which were open to visitors. Next, he unlocked the large church so that we could admire its frescoes, its enormous pulpit, and magnificent iconostasis. All of the walls of the church were adorned with frescoes except the north wall, which is blank because the pictures that were once painted on it have been obliterated by dampness. This occurred during the long period from 1969 until 1988, when the Communists closed the monastery, and then left it to decay. It was a pity that photography was forbidden in the church because there were no postcards or other reproductions of the frescoes on sale. The caretaker told us that now only two monks lived in the monastery. When Edward Lear visited it in October 1848, he was put up there for a night:

"At dusk I was taken to a most comfortable room surrounded with sofas, where for two hours or more I awaited the reverend household's performances in cookery, though I had much rather have had a simple meal at once. But at eight the Chief Papas [i.e. priest], with five or six others, entered with dishes unnumbered; pilaf, roasts, boiled, fried – fish and fruit – honey, cheese, walnuts, and wine."

The drive from Ardenicë to Berat should have been quick, but we took a long time because we tried to by-pass the town of Lushnje by using side roads that were marked on our detailed map. Unfortunately, one of them, a short critical stretch of road, was closed to traffic. Various country folk had to give us directions before we could find our way through a maze of byways through flat cultivated agricultural land to reach the road to Berat.

In Berat, we were booked at the Vila Lily, a B&B at the south-eastern end of the city near the Osumi, the river along which Berat stretches. Our B&B was close to a monstrosity that was not present in 1984: Berat University. This is housed in a neo-classical building with a huge dome reminiscent of that on Washington DC's Capitol. At the risk of sounding patronising, the building seemed to have been designed to satisfy the tastes of the uneducated *nouveaux-riches*.

We were welcomed by our hosts, Lily and Vangjeli, who insisted that we park our car within their compound for safety rather than leave it on the street. Then, Vangelj invited us sit down in his garden whilst Lili brought us cups of Turkish coffee and small dishes containing cherries in a thick sugary syrup. This reminded me of trips made to Yugoslavia and Greece, where it is traditional to welcome guests with something sweet, usually a thick sugary fruit syrup. While we were enjoying this, Vangjeli brought us some loquats that he had just plucked from one of his trees. He told us to eat them unwashed. "No chemical", he informed us. Our comfortable room had a good view of the old town in the distance. It contained a tall, old-fashioned wardrobe and a squat, glass-fronted cupboard. Perhaps, these basic furnishings, lacking in elegance, had been acquired during the Communist period.

We drove into the centre of town, parking close to the river next to a park, the 'Lulishtija'. It runs alongside a stretch of the river, and separates it from the pedestrianised section of Bulevardi Republika. When we arrived there, the sun was beginning to set. The wide boulevard was full of people wandering along it in one direction and then returning in the other. They were enjoying what is known locally as the '*xhiro*'. People of all ages, from infants in push-chairs to geriatrics in wheelchairs, take part. It is what people do of an evening in towns and villages all over southern Europe. I have taken part in it in Greece, Bosnia, Serbia, and Croatia. The *xhiro* (or '*korso*' as it is known in some parts of the Balkans) gives people a chance to relax at the end of the day, to stroll leisurely, and meet friends. We sat in one of the many cafés lining the Bulevardi, ordered some raki, and watched the world passing by. We saw women dressed up, some wearing stilettos; children in buggies or running about, or with small bicycles; groups of students; but no beggars. Across the way in the park, clusters of people, mostly older men, sat on benches chatting, playing games, or just staring vacantly at the lively evening scene. As the sun set, we watched lights coming on in the windows of the old houses on the nearby hills: a magical scene.

We had dinner in the Wildor Restaurant at the foot of the Mangalem district, which clings to the slopes of a hill crowned by the enormous acropolis or Castle of Berat. The old houses of Mangalem appear to be piled one on top of the other, which gives rise to one of the nicknames for Berat, the town of *një mbi një* (i.e. 'one on one'). From a distance, the many windows of Mangalem look like a sea of eyes staring across the valley of the Osumi, justifying another of the city's nicknames: 'City of a thousand eyes'. The name Berat is probably derived from the Slav word 'Belgrad', meaning 'white city'. Unlike the better-known Belgrade (in Serbia), Berat – especially its older sections – is filled with white-painted buildings. The town of Berat stands on the site of the Ancient Macedonian settlement of Antipatreia. The far from straight Rruga Antipatreia runs throughout the length of the city between its north-west and south-east boundaries.

The castle of Berat dominates a narrowing of the River Osumi, and made it an important place to regulate the movement of armies up and down the valley, between west and east Albania. In 200 BC, the Romans led by the consul Sulpicius camped between Apollonia and Durrës. He sent forces under his lieutenant Lucius Apustius to plunder the edges of (ancient) Macedonia. Berat was on the way. According to Livy (translated by Henry Bettenson), Apustius reached Antipatreia:

"...a town situated in a narrow defile. He began by summoning the chief citizens ... to cajole them into committing themselves to Roman protection. But, they spurned his suggestions, relying on their city's size, its fortifications, and its situation. Apustius then attacked and took the place ..., put to death all the men of military age, ..., demolished the walls and burned down the city."

By defeating this strategically important town, the Romans unblocked their route towards Macedonia.

When Edward Lear arrived in Berat in October 1848, he was impressed by its beauty and its situation:

"Berat is situated in a narrow gorge or pass of the Beratino [i.e. Osumi], which seems to have forced a passage through the tremendous rocks on either side, leaving merely a narrow space between the cliff and the water…"

Of Mangalem, he wrote:

"The city is placed chiefly on the right bank of the river, as also is the Acropolis or castle hill which rises immediately above the town – the houses and mosques are piled one above another on the steep ledges of rock which slope from the frowning fortress and its stupendous cliffs down to the water's edge, and constitutes a view that combines Tyrolean or Swiss grandeur with all the pretty etcetera of Turkish architecture."

The restaurant was owned by a pleasant woman. An architect by training, she spoke good Italian and a little English. In earlier times, she had been Berat's head city planner. We ate a good meal that included a serving of *qofte*, delicately flavoured meatballs, in tomato sauce. A former city planner was running a restaurant. She was one of many educated people whom we met, who were having to do things that they had never expected to do in life. This resulted from the ending of the Communist system, which often tried matching peoples' jobs with their education. Now that Albania has a free-market economy and greatly reduced state-financed employment, folk must forget their past experiences, and must earn a living as best they can manage.

Entrances to an underground 'Cold-War' bunker viewed from ancient Apollonia.

Near Apollonia.

Monastery at Ardenicë. Monks' quarters behind the church.

Berat, Kuçovë

Monday, 6th June 2016 We had already been served some generous breakfasts during our trip to Albania, but none could compete with what Lili served us at a table in her garden. We were presented with: fried eggs (two each), sausages (two each), homemade cheese börek ('*byrek*' in Albanian), fruitcake (home baked), tomatoes, cucumbers, white (feta-type) cheese, bread, three types of homemade jams, freshly squeezed orange juice, mountain tea (*mali çai*), and Turkish coffee. Lili also offered us a second type of *byrek* made with an egg and cheese filling, but we were replete. We finished breakfast just after 9 am.

We walked to the university, which was completely out of harmony with the rest of Berat's cityscape. This gigantic wedding-cake of a building is a 'blot on the landscape'. Nobody stopped us from entering its large vestibule, which was about three storeys high. Its gold-plated stucco ceiling was supported by fluted pillars with neo-Doric capitals. These differed from those supporting the portico outside, which had florid Corinthian capitals. The hall was clean and empty. Occasionally, someone sped across it. We stopped a lady to ask her about the place. She took us to the third floor in a lift, and directed us to an office.

There was only one person in the office, a lecturer who spoke good English. She answered our questions patiently. We learnt that the university was privately owned, a branch of an organization called 'Albanian University'. We had seen advertisement billboards for it on buildings near Skanderbeg Square in Tirana. We were told by people not associated with the university in Berat that it was set-up by a wealthy Albanian with 'connections'. The lecturer told us that the university had several faculties including an Education Department, which has one hundred and fifty students. The departments of Law, Economics, and 'Health', were all larger. We asked her where the students were on this Monday morning, as there was no sign of them in or around the building. She told us that they were at home studying because the final exams were beginning at the end of the week on Friday (they would continue over the weekend).

After speaking with the lecturer, we tried to take the lift back to the ground-floor, but it did not arrive. There had just been a power-cut. These, we learnt, were not uncommon in today's Albania, but this was the only time we were troubled by one. When we reached the ground floor, we entered the university's spacious cafeteria whose shiny floor was paved with black and white marble tiles. Several people were sitting at some of its many tables, but not drinking. We tried ordering coffees, but in vain because of the power-cut.

We left the university by its rear entrance. Lopa purchased a wide-brimmed straw sun hat from a lady whose stall was next to a dilapidated building on the edge of the university's grounds. The headwear was of the type worn by women we had seen labouring in Albania's fields. A café next door to the university had electricity, and was busy. We sat on its terrace, watching passers-by walking along the Bulevardi Republika, which in this part of the town would normally carry motor traffic had it not been under repair. Women, many of them wearing tight-fitting garments, walked past us carrying unfurled umbrellas to shade themselves from the sun.

Outside the main entrance of a school across the road, we saw a bust of Baba Dude Karbunara (1842-1917). Born in Berat, he was one of the signatories of the Declaration of Independence signed in Vlorë in November 1912. He was a teacher. During the 19th century, when the Albanian language was not permitted to be used in schools, churches and mosques, he taught children in Albanian clandestinely.

We were in the south-eastern part of Berat (the 'Lagja 30 Vjetori' district), which is less visited by tourists than the older parts around the castle. However, this 'un-touristy' section of the city with its mainly Communist era buildings was interesting because people were going about their daily business rather than catering to visitors. The roads were lined with blocks of flats peppered with satellite-TV dishes. Lines of drying laundry hung stretched across balconies. At street-level, there were well-stocked shops.

We entered a small bookstore which, like many we had visited in Albania, kept the books out of reach of customers on shelves behind the counter. So, it was necessary to ask the salesperson, in this case a friendly middle-aged lady, to pass us books that we wanted to look at. I bought a first-rate guidebook to Berat (bilingual: Albanian and English). It was part of a series of highly informative and slightly quirky guidebooks to Albanian cities published by Çelesi (Tirana). Much to the amusement of the saleslady and her friend who was sitting keeping her company, I bought an *abetare*, a colourful picture book, a primer, for teaching reading to Albanian infants. I thought that it might help me learn Albanian. Back in 1975, I bought a similar book in Prizren (Kosovo), for the same reason, but I have yet to make use of it.

There was a marketplace under a tiled canopy supported by slender metal poles. We wandered around its stalls displaying *fruta* and *perime*, fruit and vegetables. The produce was both beautiful and mouth-watering. The vendors were friendly and did not mind me taking photographs of their colourful, neatly arranged wares. One man tried explaining to us in Albanian the virtues of different kinds of capsicums. All that we could gather was that each kind of pepper had its own special role in the Albanian cuisine. One store was selling dried figs tied together on strings, just like we buy in Bangalore. Another had a box of courgettes with their large yellow flowers attached.

The market was overlooked by blocks of flats. We saw a set of ground-floor rooms opposite the market where men of all ages were playing billiards on several tables. There were other food shops close to the market: butchers, dairies, and greengrocers. These sold fresh produce rather than the ubiquitous imported packaged foods that are so often on sale in Albania.

We walked past a huge grassy field that was the site of the city's former stadium (a new one, the Stadiumi Tomori, has been built nearby), and arrived at Vila Lili, where our friendly hosts served us Turkish coffee. While we sat drinking in the garden, we spoke to two Danes who had just turned up. One of them was a professional musician, and was never without his camcorder, which he used for capturing snatches of conversation, scenery, and anything else that interested him. He told us that he would edit his films when he returned to Denmark. I have watched the movies that he made in Albania, and they are excellent. He has a good eye, and knows how to keep his viewers absorbed.

Next, we set off for Kuçovë, a town about eighteen kilometres north of Berat. Developed as an industrial centre with Italian aid in the 1920s, it became known as Qyteti Stalin (Stalin City) during the Communist period. Kuçovë used to be a centre of Albania's oil industry. The country's first oil well was sunk there in 1928. At the edge of the town, we saw a forest of abandoned, rusting oil-derricks, each with its own corroded 'nodding donkey' pump. Neighbouring this vision of desolation, there were brick and concrete industrial buildings in varying states of decay and collapse. Within these remains, small businesses were eking out a living. For example, I noticed that what was left of one wrecked building was being used as a warehouse for hanging up huge woven carpets.

When I was in Albania in 1984, I passed the oilfields near Ballsh (southwest of Berat), where some of the 'nodding donkeys' were pumping oil. At Kuçovë, there seemed to be little activity, although we learned that a Canadian company was attempting oil extraction there. The nearby airbase at Ura Vajgurore, which used to be a military airport for Albania's jet fighters, now serves as a landing ground for executive aircraft.

Most of Kuçovë was built on the slopes of a hill above the expanse of obsolete industrial structures. Stalin City was planned well with wide streets, a large central square, and a pleasant park. We parked outside the Bashkia (Town Hall) in the square (Sheshi 18 Tetori: 18th October Square). The eighteenth of October is remarkable for at least two events in Albanian history. The first in 1913 was the date that the Austrians issued an ultimatum to Serbia to remove its troops from Albania. They withdrew a week later. The second was in 1925, the day when Enver Hoxha's successor Ramiz Alia was born. Driton, our friend in Vlorë, gave the most likely reason for the square's name: on the eighteenth of October 1944, Kuçovë was liberated from the fascist forces.

The Bashkia was beside a park that extended up the slopes of a hill. At its base, we found a bust of Professor Stanisllav Zuber (1893-1947). Its plinth bore an inscription both in Albanian and Polish. The former was headed by Albania's double-headed eagle and the latter by Poland's single-headed eagle. Zuber, a geologist, was born in Lviv (Poland) and died in Tirana. He travelled to Albania in 1927, where he helped develop the oilfields in Kuçovë and elsewhere. In 1935, he settled in Albania for good and did important geological work. After the Communists assumed power, he was treated well at first, but in 1947 he was arrested and died during interrogation.

The park behind the monument contained a large café as well as a decommissioned 'nodding donkey' decoratively painted in blue and yellow, celebrating the town's erstwhile principal industry. The park abutted another green area where a long straight staircase led up to a war memorial. At the foot of the stairs to the right, there was a large cube mounted on a tall pedestal. Each of four faces of the cube had a bas-relief in the socialist-realism style. One face depicted two oil workers handling a drill; another had men in overalls dancing, one of them playing an accordion; the third had armed workers in front of an oil-derrick; and the fourth showed a woman sitting between two men, one of whom was grasping a scroll of paper.

On the other side of the steps, there was a newer monument, the bust of Astrit Suli (1976-1999). He was from the village of Lumas, northeast of Kuçovë. A soldier in the Kosovo Liberation Army, he was killed near Prizren (Kosovo) on the 27th of April, 1999. Four months earlier, he had left Greece, where he was a migrant worker, for Kosovo because he was concerned about the fate of its Albanian population.

Across the square opposite the Bashkia, we saw the former cultural centre of Kuçovë. It was locked up. A notice above one of its main doors read: "BINGO", and beside that another read: "Keshilli Sindikal I Konfederates Kuçovë" (meaning: The Trade Union Confederation Council of Kuçovë). Next to it, there was the Council's circular logo and the date 1991. A tower at the corner of the building had traces of the numerals of a clock face, but the hands were missing. A large flock of pigeons roosted on gratings covering a tall window.

We sat down for coffee under the vines that grew over the terrace of a bar next door to the cultural centre. We had a view of the centre's inner courtyard, where we noticed the entrance to a library. We entered the library, and met its six staff members. A young man, who spoke English, showed us around two rooms containing well-stocked shelves of books for readers of all ages, and told us that this is the most used public library in Albania. We were also shown a lecture hall. During the troubles that occurred in 1997 following the collapse of the pyramid schemes, angry rioters burnt the library and its books. What we were shown was the library that has grown phoenix-like from the ashes of the old one.

The cinema in the square was picturesquely painted in a variety of colours, in a way that reminded me of the work of the Dutch artist Piet Mondrian. It is still in use and named in honour of the Albanian movie star Kadri Roshi (1924 - 2007), who starred in many films between 1958 and 1998. It was built by the Italians in 1936, and having recently been restored by its private owner it now contains up-to-date projection and sound systems. A small plaque on one of its walls read (in translation): "The Kuçovë guerrilla unit shot a spy here in April 1943." By 1943, a civil war had already begun, a struggle between different Albanian resistance groups to determine who would be in a strong enough position to rule post-war Albania. There was a red Communist star above the wording on the plaque.

During our wanderings around Kuçovë, the smell of oil pervaded the air. Its oilfield is the second largest in Albania. We left what is the hottest town in Albania, and drove back to Berat.

The northern stretch of the Rruga Antipatreia, passes the ATM BKT Berat Kombinat. This huge building covers a vast area. Its multi-ridged roof can be just seen above a high enclosing wall. It was built when the Chinese were Albania's allies, and was known as the 'Mao Tse Tung Textile Factory'. Now, it has become an enterprise zone, housing various businesses. In the 1969 Albturist guidebook there is a picture of this factory (see below), which shows that then it was surrounded by countryside. Today, it has been engulfed by the expansion of the city.

The Mao Tse Tung textile factory in Berat.

(From Albturist guidebook, 1969)

Closer to the centre of the town, we examined a couple of huge WW2 memorials. One of them with two soldiers painted green and a red-painted flag, all in bas-relief, commemorated "13 Shtator 1944" (13th September 1944), the date that Communist forces liberated Berat from the Germans. The other one consisted of a giant red flag made in concrete with a black painted double-headed eagle. The flag rested against a simple white column with the words (translated): "On the 20th September 1943, the youth battalion 'Margarita Tutulani' was formed." Margarita Tutulani was born in Berat in 1924 and died in 1943. Her grandfather was a signatory of the Albanian Declaration of Independence in 1912. Aged nineteen, she and her brother Kristaq, aged twenty-four, returned from abroad, where they had been studying, to help liberate their motherland. Margarita died almost as soon as she arrived after having been first captured and then tortured by the Italians in Berat.

We crossed the Ura e Ri (New Bridge). Nowadays, it is the only of Berat's three bridges that carries vehicular traffic across the River Osumi. We arrived in Berat's Goricë district, which can also be accessed (on foot) by Berat's two other bridges. Like the much larger Mangalem district, which Goricë faces, old houses on the side of a steep hill look as if they have been piled on top of each other. Where the two districts face each other across the river, the valley is at its narrowest – it is the defile described by Livy (see above). We saw a monument to the partisan martyrs of Goricë. Margarita and Krishtaq Tutulani were amongst the ten names listed on this. We returned to the pedestrianised part of Bulevar Republik, where we enjoyed coffee and freshly baked baklava.

In the park opposite our café, there was a bust of Hajdar Tafa (1920-1950), a 'hero of the people'. Born near Berat, he joined the partisans, and after WW2 was a member of Hoxha's security forces. He was killed in 1950 while combatting anti-communist agents. Close to the tall Hotel Tomori at the southern end of the pedestrianised zone, we saw another monument to someone who had died after WW2. This one, which was not in the social-realism style, was in memory of Arben Zylyftari. He held a walkie-talkie with two stub-like antennae in his right hand. A colonel in the police, he was killed on-duty on the 2nd of August, 2000 during in a shoot-out between criminals and the police in Shkodër, where a group of miscreants, known as 'Guerrilla', were shooting people indiscriminately.

We entered the Hotel Tomori, where I stayed in 1984. Much of the building, including its rooms, have been modernised. However, the reception area and the dining room looked unchanged since the Communist era. The receptionist confirmed this. The ground floor terrace was where it was in 1984. It was here that I observed something that I thought was the stuff of spy films: a man with a newspaper peered occasionally over its pages to spy on us foreigners whilst we ate our breakfast. Where the riverside park is now, there was a small collection of market stalls in 1984, where I bought a couple of shirts made in Albania. While I was shopping, I was tailed by a not very secret-looking secret service man. The hotel used to be the only tall building in Berat, but now it has a tall new neighbour, the University of Berat.

We ate supper at a simple, but wonderful, eatery specialising in grills, run by Zani and Mira. It was near to the fruit and vegetable market, which we had visited that morning. There was an inner dining area with a large refrigerated display case, where customers selected their meat and a roadside veranda, where Zani and Mira tended a large charcoal grill like a Turkish *ocakbaşı*. We sat on the veranda, and ate over-generous portions of excellent grilled lamb and pork chops; *salce kosi*; mixed salad prepared by Mira's mother; raki; and a white wine that had a faintly resinous taste. Groups of men sat at other tables drinking beers and raki whilst awaiting the meat that they had ordered. The place did brisk business with many people coming in to collect take-away orders. By 10 pm when we walked back to the Vila Lili, the town was very quiet.

Oil workers on a Communist era monument at Kuçovë.

Berat University with three Mercedes Benz cars

Disused oil derricks and a 'nodding donkey' at Kuçovë.

Berat

Tuesday, 7 June 2016 was the first day of Ramadan. Large colourful posters attached to mosques and banners stretched across streets proclaimed the season of fasting. We drove up to Berat's extensive citadel that crowns the hill upon whose slopes the district of Mangalem perches. Encircled by walls, this 'acropolis' contains many dwellings where locals reside. From our table at a café just inside the main gateway we saw a statue of the sixteenth century fresco painter Onufri, some of whose works we had already seen in the magnificent museum in Korçë. After taking refreshment, we climbed steep streets paved with shiny, slippery cobble-stones to reach Berat's Onufri Museum. This is housed in a walled compound containing the Church of St Mary. The church, which was rebuilt in the eighteenth century, has an iconostasis with all of its icons in place, a pulpit with its characteristically conical base, and a bishop's throne. The frescoes that used to adorn the ceiling have been lost over the years, probably because of damp. I went behind the iconostasis and noticed paper labels glued on to the wooden backs of the icons. They were all handwritten and dated "1977".

A door led from the church into an adjoining building, a museum. Well laid-out and lit, it displayed many icons and some religious silverware. Some of the icons were painted by Onufri and members of his family. We were admiring these when a middle-aged Albanian with a kindly, wrinkled face spoke with us. Mehmet (not his real name) felt that things had been better during the Communist times. Everyone had had a job then, and there had been stability. His wife had had a steady job as one of the seven thousand workers at the local textile factory, and he had worked as a craftsman. Now, he had to try to eke out a living by doing odd jobs and accommodating tourists in his home for ten Euros per night. His house, near a mosque in Mangalem, was close to a minaret, from which the cries of the muezzin were broadcast every few hours, day and night. Recently, a Dutch couple had booked several nights in his home, but they left after only one night because their sleep had been disturbed by the calls to the faithful.

Mehmet worried constantly about managing to pay the high local taxes levied by the 'Bashkia' (town council) of Berat. Also, he was concerned about the poor quality of education in today's Albania. As for Berat's new private university, he, along with many others with whom we spoke, considered it to be a 'joke'. He was concerned that students were receiving diplomas, but leaving colleges with empty heads. Then, he told us that before 1990, there had been a programme for conserving and restoring the old buildings in Mangalem. A special 'Brigada', as he called it, of workers had been established to carry out this work carefully. Now, it had become a question of 'tendering'. Whoever will do the work cheapest, gets the job, and then does it badly. Mehmet was a friendly but disappointed man. Once we had met him, we kept on spotting him in Berat on his bicycle, always on the look-out for visitors to stay in his guest rooms.

While we looking at postcards and books in the museum's small shop, we chatted to a senior member of the museum's staff, who had been working there almost since it was opened in 1988. She told us that in 1967 at the time when Mao Tse Tung was fomenting his Cultural Revolution, his then ally Enver Hoxha decided that Albania should have its own. Hoxha engaged in this with great gusto, creating the world's first ever atheist state where religion was completely forbidden. To enforce this, several thousand places of worship were either demolished or used for non-religious purposes. In addition, he ordered that all religious works of art be destroyed. This might have led to the irrecoverable loss of all of Albania's religious artefacts had it not been for the efforts of several (brave) scholars. They appealed to the dictator, who was well-educated and highly interested in Albania's history, by asking him to imagine what his people would have thought of him after his death had he totally obliterated Albania's cultural heritage. In 1977, a commission of scholars was ordered to prepare an inventory of what was left of Albania's art treasures. The labels that I had seen glued to the backs of the icons in the church were part of that the inventory.

We met two young English girls at the museum. We asked them why they had decided to visit Albania. They answered that while they were at school, where they had become friends, their English teacher had given them *Broken April* by Ismail Kadare to read during a summer holiday. This was about ten years ago. They had both been so intrigued by the novel, which deals with blood-feuds in Albania, that they had vowed to visit the country one day. And, here they were, enjoying themselves. They pointed out that few youngsters visited Albania because there was now no railway connection between it and the rest of Europe. Therefore, youngsters travelling with the Eurail card that allows unlimited travel on Europe's railways, omitted visiting Albania.

Mehmet took us out of the museum by a back entrance. He guided us to Restaurant Klea, leading us down steep alleyways between picturesque old houses, with open windows and lines of drying washing stretched across balconies. I caught glimpses of the Osumi far below us, a silvery river winding snake-like between sandy banks. We drank coffee with Mehmet, and then I explored the steep uneven roads in the castle district. Its houses had tiled roofs with characteristic stone chimneys (see illustration below). Many of them had overhanging upper storeys. Only a few buildings were in bad repair. The rest looked sound, and were inhabited.

The top of the hill was occupied by the fortress proper. Hobhouse, who travelled with Byron in Albania, wrote that the town of Berat: "… is considered the stronghold of the pashalik of Vallona, and is defended by a fortress mounting forty canon."

Chimneys in Berat

I saw a few of these canons dotted about the ruins. Within the fortress's enclosing wall, I saw mostly ruined buildings, including part of a minaret. They dated back to Ottoman times. A small Orthodox Church, Shën Triadha, was perched precariously below the walls above a steep drop to the river below. The view from the walls was wonderful. The city was spread out like a map. The undulating wall of mountains beyond the river provided an impressive backdrop. In 1984, I saw the name "ENVER" spelled out on the mountainside in huge letters made from white stones. In recent years, someone has rearranged these stones so that now they spell "NEVER".

We sat on the terrace of the Restaurant Klea shaded by a trellis of vines. A couple of Finns were drinking at a table nearby. We asked them whether many of their fellow countrymen visited Albania for pleasure. They said hardly any. We ate an indifferent *Imam bayildi* and delicious fried *qofta*. The restaurant owner told me that they were made of minced veal, bread crumbs, onions, garlic, fresh mint, fresh parsley, and fresh oregano.

We returned to Goricë. While Lopa rested her bad ankle in the courtyard of a café with a *macchiato* and good view of Mangalem, I clambered along the steep lanes that wound between the old houses in the district. Many buildings were inhabited, but some (in bad condition) were empty. One locked-up, abandoned house three-storey house with larger than average windows stood near the river bank. A plaque attached to its outer wall read (in translation): "During the National Liberation war this house was a partisan base and illegally used by the (communist) party." This building was very close to a monument that included the names of Margarita and Kristaq Tutulani.

I climbed up to the outer door of the courtyard of the Church of Saint Spiridon. When I visited Berat in 1984, many in our group spotted this church from high above in the castle, and had asked our Albanian guide about it. Despite it looking just like a church, she denied that it ever had been one. The official line then was that there were no churches in Albania! When I visited it recently, it was locked up but several services are held in it every day.

Opposite it, there was a plaque on the wall of a building, which read: "Between 1902 and 1905 this was a Romanian/Vlach school with the following professors: Llambi Goxhomani, Aleksander Xhuvani, Bab Dud Karbunara, Llazar Puli, Sulo Resuli." The building that had housed the school had been the home of Spiro Megu, a lawyer.

Karbunara, whom we have already encountered, signed the Declaration of Independence in 1912. Goxhomani (1848-1924) was born in Berat, spoke several languages, and served in high places in independent Albania's Government. Alexander Xhuvani (1888-1961), born in Berat, was a scholar, a linguist whose work was appreciated by the Hoxha regime. Puli and Resuli were prominent intellectuals in Berat. Wace and Thompson wrote in *The Nomads of the Balkans*, published in 1913, that there was then a group of Vlach settlements just west of Berat. The professors listed on the plaque were all Albanians, rather than Vlachs. Tom Winnifrith wrote in *The Vlachs* that the Turks first permitted Vlach as a language for use in schools in 1905. That was three years after this school opened.

Looking up to the castle from where I was standing by the church, I saw that on one of the walls of a polygonal tower the name 'ENVER' had been written in large white letters. Lower down the vertiginous slope, which is surmounted by the castle walls, but still high above the river, stood a small Orthodox church, the Church of St Michael, which dates back to the fourteenth century. It was built next to a cave. The cave's mouth, a natural geological formation led to what appeared to be the concrete-lined entrance to a man-made tunnel or maybe, I speculated, a Hoxha-era bunker. I have since learnt that the cave used to be the home of a hermit, and that it had been lined with concrete for safety reasons. Lower down the cliff, a few feet above the river bank, there were two tunnels burrowed into the hill, and these were closed with large metal doors. Surrounded by thick concrete, these were probably entrances to cold-war era bunkers.

The views of the ranks of houses in Mangalem and the castle are best from Goricë. Here, I differ from Edward Lear, who considered that:

"… the best general views are from the side on which the castle stands."

I walked downhill towards the river bank, exploring picturesque courtyards with narrow entrances opening on to the cobbled streets of Goricë. In one of these yards shaded by overhead grape vines, there was a notice next to a large green painted front door. It stated that this house, which had belonged to Mihal Sallabanda - a local administrator during the 1940s, was one of the first bases of the LANÇ (the Communist led National Liberation Front of Albania). From what I saw of Goricë it must have been a hotbed of anti-fascist resistance during WW2. So much so that during Communist times, Goricë was re-named 'Partizani'.

We drove back across the Ura e Ri, passing the older and more attractive seven-arched Ura e Goricës, which has become a pedestrian bridge across the Osumi. Before the new bridge was built, this older crossing carried vehicular traffic. Apart from the arches that spanned the water, the bridge was provided with smaller openings that not only made it look decorative but also served as vents to reduce the impact of flash floods.

Back at the Vila Lily, we watched the sky above Berat become leaden. The grey clouds looked like overlapping scallop shells, the temperature rose, and the air became close and heavy, feeling as it does in India during the monsoons. There were rolls of thunder, which echoed between the ranges of hills enclosing the city of Berat. Lightning flashed. Flocks of birds flew hither and thither, dogs howled, and then rain pelted down dramatically. I watched the meteorological drama from our bedroom's veranda. Throughout the tempest, a sprinkler in the neighbouring garden continued spraying water upwards in pathetic competition with that plummeting from the heavens.

Ladies in Goricë (Notice the toy bear (see arrow), a dordolec *to ward off the 'evil eye')*

Berat: 6- pointed star on entrance to Teqija e Helvetive

Berat: statue of partisan heroine Margarita Tutulani with old houses of Mangalem in the background

Poliçan, Çorovodë, Osumi Canyon, Bogova, Berat

Wednesday 8th June 2016 Our excursion southwards began on the Rruga Antipatreia, where I noticed that Berat's city transport busses bore the livery of a Dutch bus company called 'Connexion', which operates bus services all over the Netherlands. The buses in Berat, like those in Vlorë (which bore an Italian transport company's livery), had been bought second-hand by the Albanians, and kept their original paintwork. Many vehicles that we saw in Albania operated with the liveries and logos of their former owners. For example, I saw a van, which once delivered goods for a bakery in Munich, driving along the streets of Korçë. It was cheaper not to respray a vehicle than to redecorate it.

We followed the River Osumi upstream, passing an isolated working military camp with camouflaged concrete buildings. The road wound up the valley crossing numerous tributaries of the Osumi. Next to many of these small bridges there were construction sites, which were associated with the building of the Trans Adriatic Pipeline. This will carry gas from Kipoi (just east of the Greek city of Alexandropolis) to Seman (a few kilometres north of Vlorë on the Adriatic). From there, it will go under the sea and resurface at the southern Italian coast south east of Lecce. This gas-carrying modern 'Via Egnatia' (or maybe it should be called 'Via Igniter') will follow the valley of the Osumi, then curve around Berat, before heading westwards towards the sea. It is part of a huge project to transport gas from Azerbaijan to western Europe.

The town of Poliçan was a pleasant surprise. We were expecting to find a drab place because of its industrial heritage. Far from it: Poliçan was a cheerful, vibrant place. We parked at the top end of the sloping triangular piazza named after the large mountain (Tomorr: 2,416 metres), which dominates the area around Berat and Poliçan. The piazza, is a right-angled triangle in plan. Its two shorter sides were lined with well-restored, freshly painted Communist-era buildings with shops and cafés. We joined the crowds drinking under colourful umbrellas outside cafés on the Rruga Miqesia, which runs off the piazza towards the town's cultural centre and Bashkia (both built in the Communist period). It was about 11 am on a working day. There seemed to be many people with sufficient time for sitting leisurely in cafés or just strolling up and down the street. A girl, who ran a mobile 'phone shop (on her own), sat with friends at a table in a café near to the shop, and only left them if a customer entered her showroom. A long out of date poster on a building advertised a meeting in Tirana for adherents of the Bektashi sect.

Near the upper end of the triangular piazza, there was a new marble monument commemorating Riza Cerova (1896-1935). He was born just south of Poliçan, and became a leading protagonist in the 'June Revolution' of 1924, when supporters of Fan Noli forced Ahmed Zogu to flee from Albania. For a brief time, Noli became Albania's Prime Minister. However, at the end of 1924, aided by the Yugoslavs and Greeks, Zogu made a counter-coup, and then assumed control the country. Soon after this, he had himself crowned 'King Zog'. Following Noli's defeat, Cerova joined the German Communist Party, and later returned to Albania where he led anti-Zogist fighters. He died during an encounter with Zog's forces.

Poliçan was important during the Communist period. It was home to an enormous arms and ammunition factory, the KM Poliçan, which was opened in 1962. This produced its own versions (the ASH-72 and ASH-82 series) of the Kalashnikov gun as well as other munitions. The factory lies amidst cultivated terraced fields on the slopes of a natural amphitheatre away from, and beneath, the southern edge of the town. Workers used to approach the factory from the town by a long staircase. We counted at least twenty-five industrial buildings in the complex, many of them with broken or missing windows. None of the numerous rusting ventilators on these edifices were emitting smoke, and there were no signs of life. The slopes surrounding the factory below were dotted with concrete and metal entrances to underground stores and tunnels. During the unrest of 1997, KM Poliçan was temporarily taken over by criminal gangs while the city was in 'rebel' hands. The factory is still used, but mainly to de-activate out-of-date Albanian weaponry. It was difficult to imagine that the peaceful scene, which we observed from a track overlooking it, had such an explosive history.

We travelled southwards through cultivated countryside and past occasional forests, always following the sinuous course of the Osumi. At the edge of Çorovodë, the administrative capital of the Skrapar District, we saw a tourist information poster beside a squat hemispherical Hoxha-era concrete bunker. It portrayed an Ottoman era bridge, which we hoped to see later. In the town's main square, there was a socialist-realism style monument: a pillar topped by a carved group: one woman with three men. One of them was holding a belt of machine gun ammunition. The base of the monument had '1942' carved in large numerals. On the 5th of

September 1942, Skrapar became the first district in Albania to be liberated from the occupying fascist forces. There was a bronze statue of Rizo Cerova in a small park next to the square. Elegantly dressed in a jacket with waistcoat, he is shown holding a rifle in his left hand. His face looked left but his tie was depicted as if it were being swept by wind over his right shoulder.

We ate a satisfying lunch in a large restaurant next to the park, the Hotel Osumi. It backed onto a fast-flowing tributary of the Osumi. After eating, we entered a café a little way upstream to ask for directions to the Ottoman bridge that we had seen on the tourist poster. We were surprised to discover a 'black' man at a table, chatting with several Albanians. He spoke perfect English, which was not surprising because he was born in Tennessee (USA). He was teaching English in Çorovodë under the auspices of the Peace Corps. With pencil and paper to hand, he was compiling his own map of the town. When we told his companions that we were trying to find the old bridge, they advised us that it was only accessible with a rugged four-wheel drive vehicle.

Driving further southwards, we reached the spectacular Canyon of the Osumi (Kanioni i Osumit, in Albanian). It is about twenty-six kilometres long, deep, and narrow. At places where the road came close to the edge of the canyon, we obtained good views. From above, it looked as if the cultivated rolling fields and pastureland had been cracked open. The crack's walls were steep sided, with dramatic striations of whitish rock. Far beneath us at the bottom of this fissure, the River Osumi flowed around its many bends. Standing at the canyon's precipitous edge, we could only hear birdsong and water rustling over the river's stony bed far below us.

Retracing our steps to Berat, we passed an abandoned building with a fading circular coloured sign painted on it. It depicted a grey cow standing between a woman in a white dress, who was writing on a clipboard, and a man in a white coat such as doctors wear. In the background, a man in an overcoat holding a shepherd's crook, was leading a flock of sheep towards the grey animal and its attendants. Around the edge of the picture, we read the words 'Stacioni Zooteknise', which literally translates as 'zoo technical station'. The building with its peeling plaster and patches of exposed brickwork had once been an animal husbandry centre.

As we drove back through Çorovodë, the sky began to cloud over, and darken. When we reached the car park close to the lower of the waterfalls at Bogovë, there were rumbles of thunder. Barely had we begun looking at some small cascades when rain began falling heavily. People sheltering at a café nearby advised us not to drive up to the higher (and more spectacular) falls during a storm.

At about 3.30 pm when we drove through Poliçan, the weather had begun to improve. However, the town that had been so lively earlier was now empty. We passed a dramatic WW2 memorial at a rural spot north of Poliçan. Its white bas-relief depicted grief-stricken boys and men in various poses. One boy held a spade. His smaller companion was holding a jug in his right hand whilst clutching an older man with his left. A man was lying dead or dying, and yet another was in the process of trying to stop himself falling backwards by supporting himself with a spade handle. His outstretched left arm was pointing at something in the distance. This tableau was a memorial to seventy-two 'workers' massacred on the 26th May 1944 by the Nazis and their collaborators. By that time, the Communist-led resistance forces were months away from victory over the Nazis. This monument recorded the vindictiveness of the Nazi occupiers, which was not confined to Albania. Recall, for example, Lidice in Czechoslovakia (where more than three hundred blameless people were shot in reprisal for Heydrich's assassination), and Oradour-sur-Glane in France (where over six hundred innocent inhabitants were murdered).

We parked outside the front of Berat's (post-1990) Orthodox cathedral of Saint Dimitri. Flanked by two bell-towers this typical Orthodox church has a large central dome. It is a far more harmonious addition to Berat's appearance than the enormous domed university. We viewed its fittings including wooden pews, whose backrests had double-headed eagles carved in them. The Orthodox Church in Albania is strictly known as 'Kisha Ortodokse Autoqefale e Shqipërisë' (the Autocephalous Orthodox Church of Albania). For leadership, it looks no further than the 'Archbishop of Tirana and all Albania'. Although its rites are typical of Orthodox Christian churches, it is autonomous, and not a 'branch' of any other Orthodox Church.

Continuing the religious theme, we visited the Lead Mosque. Some men were praying in it. When Evliya Çelebi (see above) visited it in the 17th century, he found (quoted from Robert Elsie and Robert Dankoff's edition):

"... it has a high domed roof of carved stonework covered entirely in bluish lead. It is a radiant mosque with one tall and graceful minaret which can only be compared to the minaret of the Mosque of Melik Ghazi in the town of Niksar in the eyalet of Sivas. The porticoes around the outer courtyard of this mosque have a lead roof of seven lofty domes supported by tall columns of white, polished pillars. The *medrese*, the primary school, the *tekke* and the soup kitchens have lead roofs, too."

Today, the mosque is less extensive than what the Turkish traveller saw. It has fewer domes, and occupies less space.

The fifteenth century King's Mosque (Xhamia Mbret), a short distance away, has a large covered veranda with a finely decorated wooden ceiling. The veranda was overlooked by a first-floor window with an exquisitely carved wooden balustrade. This allowed women to look down from the gallery where they must congregate. The wooden ceilings inside the mosque both above the main prayer hall and, also, above the women's gallery were elaborately carved and beautifully painted in many colours. A lattice-work screen above a sculpted, curved wooden balustrade separated the women's gallery from the main hall of the mosque. This screen allowed women to look through it without being visible to, or distracting, the men below.

A young man was crouching on the carpeted floor, wrapping small parcels in white paper serviettes. While we were sitting in the veranda, putting on our shoes after visiting the mosque, he came to us and gave us each a parcel, explaining that they contained something to eat when the fasting for Ramadan was over that day, for the *iftar*. Each of the packages contained three large, juicy dates. I am always touched when something like this happens. I remember breaking the fast with a group of Moslem traders in Bangalore, and again in London at our local store run by Palestinians. Even though it was clear that we were not of their faith, this did not deter the Moslems from sharing their *iftar* with us. To digress, I was once in a bazaar near the Howrah Bridge in Calcutta during Ramadan, when I noticed that shop-keepers were handing out portions of cooked rice to poor passers-by. When I asked one of the merchants about this, he told me that in Islam it was considered blessed to be charitable, especially during Ramadan.

The lady caretaker at the King's Mosque told us that she was a Bektashi. She led us a short distance, past some nicely carved Moslem gravestones, to the Teqija e Helvetive. This *tekke* was built in 1782 by Ahmet Kurt

Pasha, the hereditary Pasha of Berat and a contemporary of his fellow countryman Ali Pasha of Tepelenë. He was related to the Muzaka (Musachi) family that served the Ottomans until 1444 when Theodor Corona Musachi joined Skanderbeg's resistance movement. Some, but certainly not all, authorities believe that Skanderbeg's mother Voisava might have been related to the Musachi family. Others differ, suggesting she was related to a Slav family.

The *tekke* was used by the Bektashi dervishes of Berat. When the Albanian Ekrem bey Vlora (1885–1964), a signatory of the Declaration of Independence in 1912, visited it in 1908, he wrote in his diary (translated by Robert Elsie):

"Aside from the isolated prayer room, there are a number of one-storey buildings surrounded by low walls in the courtyard. These serve as accommodation for the sheikh and the dervishes ... In front of the entrance is a portico, the columns of which stem from Apollonia ... The ceiling is made up of wooden panels in such harmony as one rarely finds in Albania. The arabesques reveal not only purely Oriental elements but also clear western influence."

The last sentence chimed well with what we saw in Albania, the influence of western European art on Albanian mosque and *tekke* decoration – the Et'hem Bey Mosque in Tirana being a good example. When Pettifer wrote about the *tekke* in his 2001 guidebook, it was being used as a laboratory for restorers of historical buildings and its interior was white-washed. The white-wash has since been removed to reveal beautiful intricate frescos and strips of Arabic (or Turkish) calligraphy. The ceiling is a geometric masterpiece in carved painted woodwork. The caretaker showed us small holes made at intervals in the walls of the hall where dervishes used to whirl. They were original features placed to improve the acoustics of this lovely place.

When we were leaving the *tekke*, the caretaker told us that she was married to a Moslem (not a Bektashi), and emphasised, as many had done before, that differences in religion do not concern Albanians. She believed that 30% of Albanians are Orthodox Christians, 1% Bektashi, and the rest Moslems. An Albanian Government survey published in 2011 revealed: 57% of Albanians follow Islam; 10% Roman Catholicism; 7% Orthodox Christianity; 2% Bektashi; 5.5% 'other religions'; 2.5% atheism; and 14% preferred not to declare their religion.

There were two six-pointed stars that looked identical to Jewish Stars of David (Magen David) carved in the stone above the entrance to the *tekke*. Did these stars have any significance? A seal of Skanderbeg that I found illustrated in *Flamuri I Kombit Shqiptar* by Jaho Braha, included a double-headed eagle surmounted by a star just like a Magen David. The crest of the Musachi (Muzaka, in Albanian) family also includes a star like the Jewish one. This is a likely reason for the existence of the two stars on the *tekke*, but there might have been another one.

Some say that Berat was the final resting place of Sabbatai Sevi (1626-1676), the famous 'false-messiah'. Born Jewish in Izmir (now in Turkey), he died at Ulcinj (now in Montenegro). According to John Freely in his book *The Lost Messiah,* a masterly investigation into Sabbatai's curious life, the location of his burial place is not known for certain. Some say, he was buried in Ulcinj, but others believe that he was buried in Berat, close to the *tekke*. It was thought that his tomb existed in Berat until 1967, possibly within the *tekke* or in the graveyard between it and the King's Mosque. This is what Freely believes. However, he admitted: "... there was no concrete proof that my theory was correct, no textual reference or inscribed tombstone on the site of his grave."

There had been some graves in the *tekke* until they were destroyed in 1967, but no one knows whether one of these was Sabbatai's. The lady showing us around believed that Ahmet Kurt Pasha, who was born long after the false Messiah's death, had had an important Jewish friend, and that explained the six-pointed stars.

We bumped into Mehmet again while we were admiring the painted frescos that adorn the external walls of the Bachelors' Mosque, which stands in the lowest part of Mangalem close to the river. He was happy because he had found four tourists to hire his rooms that evening. This mosque, which we did not enter, is opposite the newish Edward Lear contemporary art gallery, which was closed. Edward Lear recorded his visit to Berat in writing and with a lovely water colour, which showed Mangalem and the castle above it. And in the foreground, he drew men in traditional costume sitting on the bank of the Osumi roughly where the Hotel Tomorri stands today.

Before returning to our guest-house, we took a final walk along the pedestrianised street, where the daily *xhiro* was beginning. We admired two nicely sculpted monuments, both busts. One depicted the bearded Baba Dud Karbunara, and the other the pretty young partisan martyr

Margarita Tutulani. The mountains surrounding the city were lit by the setting sun and partly lost in fluffy white clouds.

Poliçan: armaments factory (partial view)

Canyon of the River Osumi

Animal husbandry centre south of Çorovodë. Probably disused.

Peqin, Tirana

Thursday 9th June. We drove northeast to Peqin. In the centre of this town on the River Shkumbin, there is a mosque right next to a tall clock-tower. We parked near a sculpted bust of Mustafa Gjinishi (1912-1944). Born in Peqin, he was a Communist who worked with the British SOE in 1940. His father Adam Gjinishi had attended the raising of the Albanian flag ceremony in November 1912. Mustafa spoke English and had arrived in Albania after self-imposed exile in Yugoslavia. Roderick Bailey (see above) wrote that some thought that Gjinishi was killed by the Nazis, but:

"…it is generally believed that the attackers were Albanians and that Hoxha … had had him killed."

Hoxha's mistrust of Gjinishi can be seen his *The Anglo-American Threat to Albania*:

"Thus we parted with Mustafa Gjinishi on this occasion. However, even in the future he never became a good man, but continued his course of betrayal and remained an agent of the British."

This may explain why the monument that we saw was unlike those made in the Communist times, but of a newer design. It stands in front of the town's cultural centre, which was built by the Communists and bears the name 'Ferdinand Deda'. A son of Peqin born in 1941, Deda is a leading Albanian conductor, songwriter, and composer. He conducted orchestras used to provide music in many films produced by the Communist film production company Kinostudio Shqiperia e Re.

We sat down in one of Peqin's several cafés, and, unusually for me, I ordered Coca Cola. I was brought a tin of 'American Cola', which bore no resemblance to any Coca Cola tin that I have ever seen. However, it bore the encouraging words that it was "world choice". Made in Albania, was refreshing, but its taste had little resemblance to the 'real thing'.

On the way to the mosque, we were stopped by a policeman. Remembering 1984, an involuntary frisson of anxiety overcame me. He asked us politely in English where we were from. He had worked in London as a lift engineer in Canary Wharf for about eight years, but was repatriated because he did not have the correct documentation to remain in the UK. He reminisced about Finsbury Park and the Old Kent Road. Sadly, he and many other hardworking Albanians have had to leave the UK because they have not obtained the appropriate paperwork.

Lopa noticed an orange and cream minibus, which had the logo of 'Flughafen Hamburg'. Passengers were entering it through a door marked "EINSTEIG". It was a *furgon* that had once been used as a carrier in Hamburg Airport. Later, whilst in Peqin, I saw a bus with the turquoise blue and cream livery of the busses in which I used to travel between towns in Greece in the 1970s. The bus was of a 1970s (or earlier) design and its destination board still carried the letters (in Greek) "KTEL" (Κοινά Ταμεία Εισπράξεων Λεωφορείων), the network of regionally based companies that still operates inter-city bus services in Greece.

We were welcomed at the mosque by a young imam. He told us that during the Hoxha period the mosque and its minaret had been destroyed. All that remained was the lower part of its walls, a few courses of brickwork. Although the mosque had been demolished, the clock tower was left standing because it had no religious significance. Known as the

'Clock Mosque' (Xhamia me Sahat), it was built in 1822, destroyed in 1970, and reconstructed in 1992. Despite this, the mosque was portrayed on an Albanian 1.2 Lek postage stamp issued in March 1984. The imam spoke and understood some English, but was fluent in Arabic, which he had learnt whilst being trained at a madrassah in Saudi Arabia. The Saudis had paid for the mosque's reconstruction.

Near Paulesh (between Peqin and Elbasan) beside the Bar Restaurant Gjeli, we spotted a roadside monument dating back to the Communist era. It showed a soldier holding a rifle in his right hand. There was a pistol stuck through his trouser belt, and a flag with Albania's double-headed eagle behind him. This well-maintained, gaudily repainted, memorial recorded that on the 1st of June 1944 Mehmet Shehu, who commanded the 1st Division of the Partisans, had led an ambush on a German convoy, causing it great damage, both to the personnel and material being transported.

Mehmet Shehu was until his sudden, unexpected death in 1981 very close to Enver Hoxha in Albania's Communist hierarchy, his right-hand man and, for a time, likely successor. After he died, Shehu became a *persona non grata*. His images were removed from photographs and his family was persecuted. This monument's wording was surprising given that on the 25th of January 1982, an official order issued by Socialist People's Republic of Albania's Ministry of Education and Culture commanded the destruction of:

"...lapidars or other memorial objects related to the name of Mehmet Shehu."

I was astonished to have found a Communist monument to his wartime activity which still bore his name. I asked Michael Harrison, an expert on Albanian lapidars, about this, and his explanation was:

"As for the mention of Shehu's name the lapidar celebrates the successful attack upon a German column. If Shehu was a commander of that Brigade then to have damaged that lapidar because he had fallen out of favour would have also meant a lack of respect for those who had fought and, more importantly, died in that conflict."

We drove eastwards to the outskirts of Elbasan, where we saw the ruins of its giant metallurgical plant once again. Beside it at a road junction, I spotted something that I had seen often in Albania in 1984, but not so far on this trip. It was a horse-drawn lorry (not a wagon). Where the engine is usually located, there were horses instead. The driver sat in a cab just like that on a motorised lorry, and controlled the horses via reins that passed through holes below the windscreen into the cab, exactly where a steering wheel would be in a motorised lorry. Its load was a huge pile of hay with a man perched on top of it.

In Tirana, we handed back our trusty Tata, which had served us well. Back in London, an Indian friend remarked that in India the model of car that is most often seen broken down by the roadside is ... the Tata Indica.

After booking into our hotel (The Star), we visited the National Museum on Skanderbeg Square. Above its façade, which faces the square, there is a huge mosaic showing Albanians from various historical periods wielding a variety of weapons ranging from spears to modern guns. Behind the group, there was a red flag with a black double-headed eagle. The mosaic was made during the Communist times. When I took a picture of it in 1984, part of the red flag was superimposed with an enormous five-pointed red star outlined in white. Now, the mosaic has been altered to hide the star (see illustration below).

The museum was spacious. Each room was large enough to display exhibits without crowding them. First, we viewed a gruesome exhibition highlighting the terrors of the Communist period. Oddly, I could find no reference to the period when Albania and Mao's China were allies. There was also an exhibition, which looked new and reminded me of the 'Hello' gossip magazine: photographs of the late King Zog's family. An interesting series of rooms illustrated Albania's resistance to the fascists during WW2. Our favourite exhibit was on the second floor. Accessed through a decorative wrought-iron gate, which had to be unlocked on demand by one of the museum's guards, we viewed a magnificent collection of old icons 'collected' from churches around Albania. This was almost as spectacular as the collection housed in the Mediaeval Art Museum in Korçë.

My only criticism of the museum was that it was poorly ventilated. After spending about one and a half hours looking around it, we returned to the enormous foyer, and slumped into large comfortable armchairs located in the entrance foyer. One of the chairs was occupied by a man, who looked as if he was from the Indian sub-continent. He was working on his laptop computer. When he made a 'phone call to his wife, Lopa recognized the man's obvious Indian accent. Vijay told us that he originated in the South India, and was waiting for his son to return from cricket practice.

The National Museum (Tirana) mosaic in 1984 and 2016

We were surprised to hear that cricket was being played in Albania. Vijay told us that there was an Englishman in Tirana, who was teaching cricket to an Albanian rugby team, the recently formed (2013) Klubi Regbisë Tirana, and a match between the locals and expats (from countries where cricket is endemic) was imminent. This match between the local Albanian Eagles and the expat's team the International Lions was to be played soon after we left Albania. The Eagles, who were all out for 49, won by 1 run.

Albania almost became associated with cricket soon after gaining independence in 1912. The renowned British cricketer CB Fry (1872-1956), who was also a politician, is said by some to have been offered the throne of Albania in 1920. Fry wrote in his autobiography *Life Worth Living*:

"I do not say that I received a specific and definite invitation to become King of Albania, but … that I was well in the running for the billet."

The *Guardian* newspaper reported on the 12th August 2001 that the European Cricket Coach, Tim Dellor, first brought cricket to post-Communist Albania. The reporter concluded:

"A seed has been sown in a dusty terrain. If it grows, could a Test match take place one day in Tirana?".

Well, the Test match is still awaited, but on the 26th May 2015, Albania hosted its first ever international match. It was between the Albanian Eagles, captained by Prince Leka II, Zog's grandson, and the International Lions, captained by the English comedian Tony Hawks. The Albanian team won, and was awarded the Sir Norman Wisdom Trophy. You might wonder about the name of the trophy. During the repressive Communist dictatorship, the only foreign films that Albanians were permitted to watch were those starring the late Norman Wisdom. The *Guardian* (6th October 2010) offered an explanation of Wisdom's acceptability to Albania's Communist regime:

"Hoxha deemed that Sir Norman's films, in which his alter-ego Pitkin got the better of his bosses, were a Communist parable on class war."

It surprised us that there is an Indian community in Albania. Vijay said that there are about fifty Indians in the country. Some are nuns of the Mother Theresa Order, others are doing business or missionary work.

On our way to the National Gallery of Art, we passed the pedestrianised Shtetitorja Murad Toptani, which was filled with temporary stalls and a happy crowd enjoying an outdoor children's festival. We entered the enormous temporary art installation in front of the art gallery. It was an airy three-dimensional latticework framework of white-coloured metal rods, designed by the Japanese architect Sou Fujimoto. Rather like a climbing frame or a magnified three-dimensional Sudoko puzzle without numbers, the installation in Tirana resembled that which Fujimoto designed for the temporary summer pavilion at London's Serpentine Gallery in 2013.

On entering the art gallery, a man approached us, and offered us assistance in perfect English. He was a senior official at the National Gallery of Art, who had studied at English universities. I showed him a picture of a sculpture that I had taken at the gallery in 1984. He looked at the image, and then asked us to follow him. He led us to a yard behind the gallery. There, I saw the sculpture which I had photographed in 1984. It was not alone. It stood alongside two larger than life bronze statues of Joseph Stalin and one of Lenin. The statue of Lenin was the first sculptural portrait of this man to have been made in Albania. Amongst the statues there was something resembling an oversized chess pawn. Covered with an opaque sheet secured firmly with cords this 'package' contained the bust of someone who had upset and killed many Albanians for over forty years. Too many peoples' sensitivities would have been disturbed had Enver's sculpted head been left uncovered.

We asked our companion if he believed that everything had been bad in Albania under Enver Hoxha, because we had heard from other people that life under the dictator had had some advantages. He told us that he credited Hoxha with dragging Albania kicking and screaming into the twentieth century. For example, he gave women equal rights and gave rights to the Roma people living in the country.

Berat: Ladies' gallery in the King's Mosque

Peqin: a lady and her carpets.

Near Elbasan: a horse-drawn lorry with driver's cab.

Tirana

Friday 10th June 2016 Bujar accompanied us to the National Museum, where I presented its librarian with a copy of each of my two books, *Albania on my Mind* and *From Albania to Sicily*, to be placed in the library. We also donated copies of these to the National Library of Albania. Then, we visited a well-equipped room in that library, the 'American Corner', which has been financed by the Government of the USA. Filled with American publications and comfortable furniture, the room was dominated by a disconcertingly realistic, life-size, cardboard cut-out photograph of President Barack Obama.

We walked with Bujar past the newly unveiled Friendship Monument, a colourful object financed by the Kuwaitis, which looked as if it has been made with oversized chocolate 'Smarties'. On the way to a restaurant in the Bllok, we kept meeting people who stopped to chat with our host. Surrounded by a garden, this fashionable, elegant modern eatery was comfortable and well-appointed. We ate a range of traditional Albanian dishes, including meat in a rich yoghurt and tomato sauce, and *tava kosi*.

In 1984, when I visited Albania, material conditions were at their very worst in the country, but this was not at all evident to me (or others in our tour group) at the time. I was completely unaware of the appalling conditions that the locals were having to endure. Bujar told us that in the Hoxha period, places that were to be visited by foreigners were especially prepared and 'spruced up' a few days before the visitors arrived. When they arrived, there would always be a black Volga limousine parked nearby. It would have been filled with security men, who were there to observe and report what happened during the visit. What our tour group had been shown in 1984 was an elaborate hoax, a large-scale Potemkin Village, set up to distract us from the harsh realities of life in Albania.

During Communist times, it was not only physical discomforts that people suffered. Everything else was difficult, even marrying. Bujar told us about a man who wanted to marry the daughter of a senior military officer. The aspiring groom had a relative who had left Albania to live in the USA before WW2. In the eyes of the authorities having a relative who lived abroad, especially in the USA, made his whole family 'unreliable, or 'tainted'. On the other hand, senior military men were only picked from the most 'reliable' families. The aspiring bride met great opposition to marriage from her family. Had she married the man with a relative in the USA, her family would have become 'unreliable' in the eyes of the authorities. Bujar knew of one girl from an 'unreliable' family who had married a military man. A few months after the marriage, the groom was thrown out of the army.

While dishes kept arriving at our table, we discussed the simultaneous use of two currencies in Albania. Throughout our journey, we had been quoted prices both in Euros and in Albanian Leks. Both were acceptable and there was no financial advantage to us in preferring one over the other. Bujar suggested that the situation was not good for the economy of the country because of the impossibility of keeping track of the flow of the two currencies.

After lunch, we met our Indian friend Vijay along with his wife and children at a café outside the Opera House. Vijay's wife had brought along some Indian snacks that she had cooked for us: spiced potato *bhajis* (patties) and chicken tikka. While we were sitting with this delightful family, Vijay spotted another Indian walking towards us. We were introduced to Vicky, who was working at the time in the Tirana office of an Indian mining company in Albania. He shared Bujar's concerns about Albania's parallel use of two currencies. He said that until the Euro is accounted for officially, Albania's economic problems will be difficult to resolve.

That evening at the Opera, we attended Tchaikovsky's ballet *The Nutcracker*. Performed by an Albanian ballet company, it was excellent. The dancing was delicate, the settings magical, the music well-performed: a dreamlike show.

Ballet in Tirana: "The Nutcracker"

Tirana: larger than life statue of Josef Stalin.

Tirana

Saturday 11th June 2016 was the last day of our sojourn in Albania. At the corner of Rruga e Dibrës and Rruga Barrikadave on the edge of a small park, we found a shoe-shine man. We asked the price of polishing my shoes, which had become unkempt during our adventures. The man wrote "20" on a scrap of paper. That seemed cheap. He polished my shoes meticulously, and then we handed him twenty Lek in coins (about twelve UK pence before the British voted to leave the EU). He refused to take them, repeatedly saying: "No metalli". We kept trying to offer him the coins, and he kept repeating "No metalli". Then, he said what sounded like: "Jo metalli, letër, letër…" (i.e.: no metal, paper, paper…), and suddenly the 'penny dropped'. We realised that he wanted banknotes, not coins. He had written '20' instead of '200'. Possibly, this was he had not yet adjusted to some previous currency redenomination. He was content with the latter amount.

Walking past various pre-Communist era buildings, which are still standing in a city where demolition and new construction continues apace, I hoped that these old buildings will survive to help preserve the charm of the city of Tirana.

We arrived at the narrow Rruga Vildan Luarasi. This street contains the Sali Shijaku House, which, like so many old Tirana homes, is surrounded by walls. Its outer doors were opened by Mrs Shijaku, the daughter-in-law of the artist Sali Shijaku.

Sali was born in 1933 in Tirana, and lives in the spacious, beautiful old Ottoman style mansion with his son, who is also an artist. We were shown around the house. Its walls were lined with framed paintings by Sali. I would happily hang any of these in our home. The house retains many of its original architectural features including wooden staircases leading to upper floors and an airy roof space criss-crossed with wooden supporting beams.

The artist and his family were permitted to keep their roomy home throughout the Communist period, a time when many families were forced to move from their large family homes into smaller cramped living quarters. Sali was allowed this because his art pleased the Hoxha regime.

Like the great painters of church images, who had to work within the framework of Christian precepts, Sali created great art within the constraints imposed by the doctrine of Albania's Communist rulers. Honoured by the state as a 'People's Painter', Shijaku managed to paint what was 'required' without compromising his fine artistic talent. Although many of his paintings from the period of dictatorship contained 'approved' subject matter, Sali depicted it in an original way that made his work stand out from the standard socialist-realism style that dominated Albanian art during those times. I do not condemn the art done in this style, because much of it demonstrates high technical and artistic standards, but Sali's works from that difficult time (and after it) have proved him to be an exceptionally talented, original artist. After the end of Communism, his range of subject matter expanded to include subjects (including nudes) that would not have been tolerated in the past.

We entered the garden, where I spotted a tortoise scuttling about. We had seen many of these during our drive through rural southern Albania. Often, we saw them risking death trying to cross roads. A new wing of the house, looking out over the garden, contained an attractive space for serving refreshments, but this was closed during our visit. Near the outer gate, a staircase led down to a well-maintained underground bunker left over from the Communist period. A sign on the wall of the staircase read: "N.OFICERI ROJES PPSH" (Guard Officer, PPSH [Worker's Party of Albania]). And at the bottom of the stairs another painted sign proclaims "Glory to the PPSH" in Albanian. To recapture the atmosphere of the olden days, some ex-army militaria had been hung on a coat rack within the bunker.

We walked to where the old, recently demolished, railway station of Tirana once stood, at the north end of Bulevar Zogu I. When I visited Tirana in 1984, this wide street was called Shtetitorja Dëshmorët i Kombit (Promenade of the Martyrs of the Nation). It was re-named in 2000. A statue of King Zog stands in the square at the north end of 'his' *bulevar*. We sat in a lively café within view of it. A man wandered past banging a large drum. People were out walking their dogs. Cars pulled up by the pavement to drop off passengers, and then re-joined the busy Saturday morning traffic.

Moustachioed Zog, whose face reminded me of a dentist with whom I once worked, stood on a pedestal, his jacket bedecked with medals, his hands resting on the hilt of a long sword. Zog, dictator and self-appointed King of Albania, ruled his country between 1925 and 1939 with much financial and other help from the Italians, from whom he fled (taking with him much of Albania's gold) when they invaded his country in 1939. There is meagre support for the royal family in Albania. King Zog does not usually get much praise as a ruler. There was much wrong with his career, but he ought not be condemned out of hand. The historian Joseph Rothschild wrote of Zog in his book *East Central Europe between the Two World Wars*:

"On balance, to have in two short decades consolidated the new Albanian state against the pulls of regionalism and tribalism, against the pressure of the *frondeur* and brigand tradition, against the corrosions of mass poverty and illiteracy, and against the hazards of an international system that allowed predatory neighbours to deny the very legitimacy of an independent Albania was a creditable political achievement."

Statue of King Zog in Tirana

The Albanian historians Stefanaq Pollo and Arben Puto, writing in Albania in 1981 during Hoxha's rule, said of the king:

"... Zogu's régime ... brought with it a kind of stability. It is said that it was the most stable government Albania had had since its proclamation of independence. But it was the worst possible kind of stability. For what the country needed most of all was to develop and progress, whereas the régime put all its effort into keeping it in its past state of narrow dependence – an archaic and ignorant state."

Well, something like this might one day also be written about Zog's successor, Enver Hoxha.

Another man, somewhat dishevelled in appearance, banging a drum, wandered casually past our café just before we left. We reached Skanderbeg Square a little early for our next rendezvous. So, we strolled around it, passing the National Bank of Albania, an elegant pre-WW2 Italian fascist building with a curved façade, neatly clad with thin red bricks. Near it, we came across the Teatri I Kukullave, a small puppet theatre catering for children. Like the Opera across the square, its ticket office had limited, short daily opening hours. Around the corner from it, we saw a bookshop-cum-café called Librari Agolli. Located close to the headquarters of Albania's Socialist Party, this is one of the last remaining of the many small bookshops that used to be found in Tirana. The café looked active enough, but the bookshop, which was closed, looked old-fashioned and 'tired'. Dritëro Agolli, a writer (of novels and poetry) born in 1931, was a leading figure during the Communist period. He became a member of the Socialist Party after 1991, and served as a Member of the Albanian Parliament for a while.

Back in the square, I noticed one of Tirana's many orange-coloured articulated busses (like the 'bendy busses' that clogged up London's streets for a few years) passing in front of the former Palace of Culture. It reminded me that in 1984, articulated busses, coloured red, were amongst the very few motor vehicles that could be seen on Tirana's, then very quiet streets. This memory prompted another. It was of a bus station somewhere in Albania, where I saw a bus 'packed to the gills' with passengers hanging onto its exterior, like some local busses I have seen (and travelled on) in India. Today, in Tirana busses are packed at rush hour, but not like what I saw in '84.

We met Vijay and Vicki outside the National Museum. Soon, a small car turned up, and we all piled inside. It was driven by another member of Albania's small Indian community. Father Oscar, a priest born in western India, heads up the large Don Bosco Centre in Tirana, which is home to a variety of important educational and social establishments. A branch of the worldwide Roman Catholic order, founded in the 1870s to bring education to the poor, the Tirana institution was opened soon after the end of Communism. Its premises are on a street named after its founder, and caters for several thousand Albanian students.

We drove to a suburb of Tirana, where Vijay and his family have an airy apartment near some Hoxha period industrial buildings. Waiting for us, there was something that I had never remotely imagined we would be offered in a private house in Albania: an Indian buffet. It included: chicken *biryani*; *dal*; chicken curry; *channa* (chickpeas); and *rotis* fresh from the *tava* (hotplate). Vijay's wife had done us proud with her superb cooking. The animated chat and laughter around the table transported me back to many such gatherings that I have enjoyed in India. Eating homemade Indian food with an Indian family living in Tirana was even more unexpected than visiting an Israeli café in Vlorë.

After lunch, Father Oscar drove us along silent streets to bring us to Tirana's Roman mosaic. The streets were deserted because Albania was engaging Switzerland in a Euro Football match. The mosaic, surrounded by a thin wire fence, was closed. This did not matter because most of the 3rd century AD mosaic could be seen easily by looking over or through the low fence.

Father Oscar dropped us back at Skanderbeg Square, and we headed towards the pedestrianised Murat Toptani, which had become extremely lively. A crowd of people were sitting at tables or standing near them. Everyone had tense expressions, all eyes were focussed on an outdoor screen on which a TV broadcast of the Albania vs Switzerland match was being projected. Many of the crowd had Albanian flags draped over their shoulders and some were wearing traditional white felt, dome-shaped Albanian headwear (*qeleshe* in Albanian). Others were sporting base-ball caps. Some of the spectators were drinking beer out of plastic beakers, supplied at regular intervals by waiters from the nearby cafés. Whenever anything even remotely interesting happened on the screen, everyone rose to their feet and shouted. The excitement was infectious, even for me – and I have almost no interest in football.

We escaped from the noisy gathering by entering the pleasant gardens of the nearby Kinema Millenium, where we were served coffee by a lackadaisical waiter, whose mind was more on soccer than service. The cinema, which was first opened in 1996 and then subsequently modernised after 2000, was housed in what was once the Pallati i Pioniereve (Pioneers' Place). It used to contain a theatre for artistic performances. By the end of the 1990s there were nine cinemas in Tirana, including the Millenium.

The Albanian cinema industry thrived in the years of Communism. Many films were made, most of them of a high cinematographic standard, and all of them 'on-message' with Hoxha's brand of Marxism-Leninism. Countless reels of film made in the years of dictatorship lie rotting slowly in storage shelves. Fortunately, an attempt is being made to restore and preserve them by an organisation called the Albanian Cinema Project. I have discovered that many Albanian films made during the Hoxha years may be viewed 'on-line' on 'Youtube'. They give an idea of both the high cinematographic quality of these productions, and of what the Communists believed would educate and entertain the people, who were forbidden from watching films made outside the country, apart from films starring the English comedian Norman Wisdom (see above).

Albania lost to Switzerland. The hot streets became quiet, subdued. We walked towards the Sheshi Avni Rustemi, a circular open space. Avni Rustemi (1895-1924), a teacher, was an Albanian nationalist, and after independence a Member of the Albanian Parliament. On the 13th of June 1920, he assassinated a political rival Essad Pasha Toptani in Paris. Rustemi returned to Albania as a hero, but was murdered four years later in Tirana. It was believed that Zog (later to become king) had ordered Rustemi's death as a vengeance killing. Rustemi's well-attended funeral was the prelude to the 1924 revolution that made Fan Noli the country's leader briefly. In the middle of the *sheshi*, mounted on a pedestal we saw the bust of Rustemi. Dressed in a suit with shirt and tie, he was described by the plaque on the plinth as a 'Hero of the People'.

I explored a large covered fruit and vegetable market occupying one quadrant of the *sheshi*. It was not nearly as clean as that which we saw in Korçë. Apart from the expected displays of fresh fruit and vegetables, as well as tubs of tempting olives, there were some stores selling multi-coloured packages placed alongside what resembled golden-brown loaves of bread. These loaves were not bread, but compressed tobacco. They rested on large plastic bags filled with white filter tips for inserting into home-rolled cigarettes. The tobacco was Albanian, grown around Shkodër. The colourful boxes also contained tobacco. Several of them bore the brand name 'Tarabosh', which is the name of a mountain close to Shkodër.

After dinner, we returned to the café next to our hotel, and bid farewell to Tirana by downing some tiny glasses of raki. I always find it difficult leaving a place, which I like. Leaving Albania proved to be a great wrench. Everyone we met had been kind and friendly to us. Everything that we saw and experienced has made us want to return to the 'Land of Eagles' soon.

'Loaves' of tobacco (Tirana)

Tirana: Albania plays Switzerland

Gjirokastër: view over the Old Bazaar

Looking both ways

Albania's eagle, its national symbol, has two heads. One looks left, the other right; or, maybe east and west; or past and future. In this book, I have looked not to the future, which is difficult to predict, but to Albania's present and the past, which are inextricably intertwined.

On learning that I had visited the country in 1984, many people we met in Albania asked me if it had changed for the better. The answer is 'yes'. In 1984, the country was as beautiful as it is now, but most people were living in dreadful conditions. Despite what people told us about the stability of life under the Communists and nostalgia for the 'good old days', this stability if it existed at all was fragile. One false move, whether intentional or more often unintentional, could send someone to a prison camp or worse, and bring great difficulties for his or her family.

Today, life for Albanians is filled with uncertainty; but they can worship the way they want; they can say what they think; write and read anything; they can travel where they wish; work abroad; and do not starve. The only constraint on today's Albanians is economic. The country is still amongst the poorest in Europe, but no one is preventing enterprising Albanians from trying to improve their lot.

In 1984, the only Albanians with whom I could speak were the two Albturist guides and our coach driver, a well-educated member of the Albanian Communist Party. During our recent trip, my wife and I were free to speak with any Albanian who wished to converse with us, and no one we met was tongue-tied. Whatever language barriers there were between us and them, Albanians made a great effort to understand us and to make themselves understood. Almost without exception, people were warm and exceptionally kind to us. Albanians overflow with kindness and hospitality.

Albania shed the tyranny of dictatorship in late 1990. Its entry into the modern 'free' world was not easy. Difficulties included: complex internal politics; the Pyramid Schemes and the civil war that followed their collapse; the violent disintegration of their neighbour the former Yugoslavia; and then the Kosovo crisis. Many Kosovan refugees flooded into Albania at a time when the country was ill-prepared to look after them, but Albanian hospitality ensured that the Kosovans were not let down.

Today, Albania is modernising. Internet coverage is better than in some parts of the UK. Roads are being modernised. Much building work is being done. Every bar and café has at least one wide-screen television. Old towns are being brought up to date. We saw fine examples of that at Poliçan and in Përmet. Yet, all of this is happening in what might be described as the world's largest archaeological site, namely the ruins of the era of Enver Hoxha. Wherever we went, we saw relics from this period: bunkers, factories, railways, mines, and monuments. Many of these are reminders of the notion that was in Hoxha's mind: to modernise Albania, yet keep it truly self-sufficient and self-reliant without straying from his own brand of 'Marxism-Leninism'. At least Hoxha, unlike the leaders of another isolationist nation North Korea, did not feel it necessary to become a threat to the outside world.

The Communist era monuments ('lapidars') were an unending source of fascination to me. Not only were they often interesting artistically, but also they reflected local attitudes to the not so distant past. Some monuments have been left to decay, others have been defaced with graffiti. However, many of them appear to have been well-maintained. These mementos record lives lost, local men and women who died during the struggle to rid Albania of its fascist invaders. They commemorated the loss of people fighting on the side of the Communists. Gradually, memorials are appearing to remind Albanians of their many fellow citizens who became victims of the Communists. The grisly exhibition in the National Museum in Tirana goes some way towards addressing this tragedy.

On both trips that I have made to Albania, I have been impressed by the country's great beauty. In 1984, our tour group was taken where the government-controlled travel company dictated, and unsurprisingly we were shown beautiful places. On our recent trip, we went wherever we wished, and everywhere we visited was without exception very beautiful. It is amazing that such a small country as Albania can contain so much exceptionally wonderful and endlessly varying scenery. Yet, it does. And, this fantastic landscape is filled with wonders: historical, folkloric, and geological. We travelled through a land peopled with kind helpful folk, all of whom gave us a warm welcome.

I hope that this book will encourage others to visit Albania. As the young girl in Korçë said to us: "Lezzgo!"

Tirana: Statue of Skanderbeg.

Note the pre-WW2 Italian-built government buildings behind.

Acknowledgements

I wish to thank everyone in Albania who helped make our trip so enjoyable. I have altered the names of some of these people because even today in Albania opinions that might be considered innocent can give rise to argument. I have included what they told me because I felt that it would help give readers a more balanced view of the country. I would also like to thank Michael Harrison and Edward Langille. Above all, I am grateful to my wife Lopa for being such a wonderful, enthusiastic travelling companion and for her encouragement whilst writing this book.

SOURCES

I consulted many books while writing this one. I have mentioned some, but not all of them, in the text and, also, in my reading list (see below). The Internet proved to be a mine of useful information. Wherever possible I have tried to cross-check what I have discovered there with other sources. However, undoubtedly some factual errors or disputed opinions may have crept into my text. I hope that these will not cause offence or dismay. Naturally, any faults in my text are my sole responsibility, and I beg the reader's forgiveness for them.

SOME FURTHER READING

ABRAHAMS, F. *Modern Albania* (publ. 2015)

ACADEMY OF SCIENCES OF THE PEOPLE'S SOCIALIST REPUBLIC OF ALBANIA. *The Earthquake of April 18, 1979 and the Elimination of its Consequences* (publ. 1983)

ALBTURIST. *Tourist Guidebook of Albania* (publ. 1969)

BAILEY, R. *The Wildest Province: SOE in the Land of the Eagle* (publ. 2009)

BROWN, A. *The Rise & Fall of Communism* (publ. 2009)

BYRON, G. *Childe Harold's pilgrimage* (publ. 1812-18)

DURHAM, ME. *High Albania* (publ. 1909)

ELSIE, R. *Historical Dictionary of Albania* (publ. 2010)

FEVZIU, B. *Enver Hoxha: The Iron Fist of Albania* (publ. 2016)

FREELY, J. *The Lost Messiah: In Search of the Mystical Rabbi Sabbatai Sevi* (publ. 2001)

HITCHENS, C. *The Missionary Position: Mother Teresa in Theory and Practice* (publ. 2014)

HOBHOUSE, JC. *A journey through Albania and other provinces of Turkey in Europe and Asia during the years 1809 and 1810* (published 1817)

JACQUES, E & YOUNG, D. *Battle for Albania* (publ. 1998)

KADARE, I. *Albanian Spring: The Anatomy of Tyranny* (publ. 1991)

KADARE, I. *Broken April* (publ. 1978)

KADARE, I. *Chronicle in Stone* (publ. 1971)

KADARE, I. *The Concert* (publ. 1988)

KADARE, I. *The Successor* (publ. 2003)

KNIGHT, EF. *Albania: A Narrative of Recent Travel* (publ. 1880)

LEAR, E. *Journals of a Landscape Painter in Greece and Albania* (publ. 1851)

LUBONJA, F. *Second Sentence: Inside the Albanian Gulag* (publ. 2009)

LUBONJA, F. *The False Apocalypse: From Stalinism to Capitalism* (publ. 2014)

MAHUZIER, A. *L'Albanie entrouvre ses frontiers* (publ. 1965)

MANN, S. *Albanian Literature* (publ. 1955)

OAKLEY-HILL, D. *An Englishman in Albania* (publ. 2002)

PARANGONI, I. *Between Glory and Fall* (publ. 2015)

PEACOCK, W. *Albania: The Foundling State of Europe* (publ. 1914)

PETTIFER, J & VICKERS, M. *The Albanian Question: reshaping the Balkans* (publ. 2009)

PETTIFER, J. *Blue Guide to Albania (and Kosovo)* Various editions: 1994, 1996, & 2001

PHILBY, K. *My Silent War* (publ. 1968, republ. 2002)

PLLUMI, Z. *Live to Tell* (publ. 2008)

POLLO, S, & PUTO, A. *History of Albania: From Its Origins to the Present Day* (publ. 1981)

POUQUEVILLE, FCHL. *Travels in Epirus, Albania, Macedonia, and Thessaly* (English translation publ. 1820)

ROSELLI, A. *Italy and Albania: Financial Relations in the Fascist Period* (publ. 2006)

SEBBA, A. *Mother Teresa* (publ. 1997)

VARIOUS AUTHORS. *Architetti e ingegneri italiani in Albania* (publ. 2012)

WACE, A & THOMPSON, M. *The Nomads of the Balkans* (publ. 1913)

WARD, P. *Albania* (publ. 1983)

WINNIFRITH, TJ. *The Vlachs: The history of a Balkan people* (publ. 1987)

Some more books are listed in "Albania on my Mind" by Adam Yamey (publ. 2012)

Fresco in Et'hem Bey Mosque in Tirana